PONTIFICIUM CONSILIUM
AD CHRISTIANORUM UNITATEM FOVENDAM

DIRECTORY FOR THE APPLICATION OF PRINCIPLES AND NORMS ON ECUMENISM

CTS Publications

First published 1993 by the
Incorporated Catholic Truth Society
38-40 Eccleston Square
London SW1V 1PD

© 1993 The Incorporated Catholic Truth Society

ISBN 0 85183 890 1

Printed by The Ludo Press Ltd, London SW18 3DG

TABLE OF CONTENTS

PREFACE

I

THE SEARCH FOR CHRISTIAN UNITY

II

THE ORGANIZATION IN THE CATHOLIC CHURCH
OF THE SERVICE OF CHRISTIAN UNITY

III
Ecumenical Formation in the Catholic Church

IV
Communion of Life and Spiritual Activity
among the Baptized

V
ECUMENICAL COOPERATION
DIALOGUE AND COMMON WITNESS

PREFACE

1. The search for Christian Unity was one of the principal concerns of the Second Vatican Council. The Ecumenical Directory, called for during the Council and published in two parts, one in 1967 and the other in 1970,[1] "has given a most valuable service in directing, coordinating and developing the ecumenical effort".[2]

Reasons for this Revision

2. Besides the publication of the Directory, numerous other documents that have a bearing on ecumenism have been published by competent authorities.[3]

The promulgation of the new *Code of Canon Law* for the Latin Church (1983) and of the *Code of Canons of the Eastern Churches* (1990) has created in ecumenical matters a disciplinary situation for the faithful of the Catholic Church which is partly new.

In the same way, "The Catechism of the Catholic Church" recently published (1992), includes the ecumenical dimension as part of the basic teaching for all the faithful of the Church.

3. Furthermore, from the time of the Council onwards fraternal relations with Churches and ecclesial Communities which are not in full communion with the Catholic Church have intensified; theological dialogues have been set up and

---

[1] Secretariat for Promoting Christian Unity (SPCU), *Ecumenical Directory, Ad Totam Ecclesiam, AAS* 1967, 574-592; *AAS* 1970, 705-724.

[2] *Address* of Pope John Paul II to the Plenary Session of the Secretariat for Promoting Christian Unity, February 6, 1988, *AAS* 1988, 1203.

[3] Among these are the Motu Proprio *Matrimonia Mixta, AAS* 1970, 257-263; *Reflections and Suggestions concerning Ecumenical Dialogue*, SPCU, *Information Service* (IS) 12, 1970, pp. 5-11; the *Instruction on Admitting Other Christians to Eucharistic Communion in the Catholic Church, AAS* 1972, 518-525; a *Note about certain interpretations of the Instruction concerning particular cases when other Christians may be admitted to Eucharist communion in the Catholic Church, AAS* 1973, 616-619; the document on *Ecumenical Collaboration at the Regional, National and Local Levels*, SPCU, IS 29, 1975, pp. 8-31; Pope Paul VI, Apostolic Exhortation *Evangelii Nuntiandi* (EN), 1975; John Paul II Apostolic Constitution *Sapientia Christiana* (SapC) on Ecclesiastical Universities and Faculties, 1979; John Paul II Apostolic Exhortation *Catechesi Tradendae*, 1979; and the *Relatio Finalis* of the Extraordinary Synod of Bishops, 1985; *Ratio Fundamentalis Institutionis Sacerdotalis* of the Congregation for Catholic Education, Rome, 1985; the Apostolic Constitution *Ex Corde Ecclesiae, AAS* 1990, 1475-1509.

have increased in number. In his discourse to the plenary session of the Secretariat (1988), which was dedicated to the revision of the Directory, the Holy Father noted that "the breadth of the ecumenical movement, the multiplication of dialogue statements, the urgent need that is felt for a greater participation by the whole People of God in this movement, and the consequent necessity of accurate doctrinal information, in view of a proper commitment, all of this requires that up-to-date directives be given without delay".[4] It is in this spirit and in the light of these developments that the revision of this Directory has been made.

To Whom is the Directory Addressed

4. The Directory is addressed to the Pastors of the Catholic Church, but it also concerns all the faithful, who are called to pray and work for the unity of Christians, under the direction of their Bishops. The Bishops, individually for their own dioceses, and collegially for the whole Church, are, under the authority of the Holy See, responsible for ecumenical policy and practice.[5]

5. At the same time it is hoped that the Directory will also be useful to members of Churches and ecclesial Communities that are not in full communion with the Catholic Church. They share with Catholics a concern for the quality of ecumenical activity. It will be an advantage for them to know the direction those guiding the ecumenical movement in the Catholic Church wish to give to ecumenical action, and the criteria that are officially approved in the Church. It will help them to evaluate the initiatives that come from Catholics, so as to respond to them adequately, and will also help them better to understand the Catholic responses to their initiatives. It should be kept in mind that the Directory does not intend to deal with the relations of the Catholic Church with sects or with new religious movements.[6]

Aim of the Directory

6. The new edition of the Directory is meant to be an instrument at the service of the whole Church and especially of those who are directly engaged in ecumenical activity in the Catholic Church. The Directory intends to motivate, enlighten and guide this activity, and in some particular cases also to give binding directives in accordance with the proper competence of the Pontifical Council for

---

[4] *AAS* 1988, 1204.
[5] cf. *CIC*, can. 755; *CCEO*, can. 902 and 904, 1. In this Directory the adjective *catholic* refers to the faithful and to the Churches that are in full communion with the Bishop of Rome.
[6] See Nos. 35-36 below.

Promoting Christian Unity.[7] In the light of the experience of the Church in the years since the Council and taking account of the present ecumenical situation, the Directory brings together all the norms already established for implementing and developing the decisions of the Council given up to the present and brings them up to date when necessary. It strengthens the structures that have been developed for the support and guidance of ecumenical activity at every level of the Church. While fully respecting the competence of authorities at different levels, the Directory gives orientations and norms of universal application to guide Catholic participation in ecumenical activity. Their application will provide consistency and coordination to the various practices of ecumenism by which particular Churches [8] and groups of particular Churches respond to their different local situations. It will guarantee that ecumenical activity throughout the Catholic Church is in accordance with the unity of faith and with the discipline that binds Catholics together.

In our day there exists here and there a certain tendency to doctrinal confusion. Also it is very important in the ecumenical sphere, as in other spheres, to avoid abuses which could either contribute to or entail doctrinal indifferentism. The non-observance of the Church's directives on this matter creates an obstacle to progress in the authentic search for full unity among Christians. It is the task of the local Ordinary and of the Episcopal Conferences and Synods of Eastern Catholic Churches to see to it that the principles and norms contained in the Ecumenical Directory are faithfully applied, and with pastoral concern to take care that all possible deviations from them are avoided.

[7] Apostolic Constitution *Pastor Bonus* states:

"Art. 135: The function of the Council is to concentrate in an appropriate way on initiatives and ecumenical activities for the restoration of unity among Christians.

Art. 136: (1) It sees that the decrees of the Second Vatican Council which pertain to ecumenical matters are put into pratice. It deals with the correct interpretation of the principles of ecumenism and mandates their execution. (2) It fosters, brings together, and coordinates national and international Catholic organizations promoting the unity of Christians, and it is watchful over their initiatives. (3) After having first consulted with the Supreme Pontiff, it looks after relations with Christians of Churches and ecclesial Communities which do not yet have full communion with the Catholic Church, and especially establishes dialogues and talks for promoting unity with them, carrying out the work with trained experts of proven theological doctrine. It deputes Catholic observers for Christian meetings and invites observers from other Churches and ecclesial Communities to Catholic gatherings whenever it seems appropriate.

Art. 137: (1) Since the matters dealt with by this department often by their nature touch on questions of faith, it must proceed in close connection with the Congregation for the Doctrine of the Faith, especially when it is a matter of publishing public documents and declarations. (2) In carrying out matters of major importance, however, which concern the separated Eastern Churches, it must first consult the Congregation for the Eastern Churches.

[8] Unless otherwise indicated, the term *particular Church* is used throughout this Directory to indicate a diocese, eparchy or equivalent ecclesiastical territory.

Outline of the Directory

7. The Directory begins with a declaration of the commitment of the Catholic Church to ecumenism (Chapter I). This is followed by an account of the steps taken by the Catholic Church to put this commitment into practice. It does this through the organization and formation of its own members (Chapters II and III). It is to them thus organized and formed, that the provisions of Chapters IV and V on ecumenical activity are addressed.

I. *The Search for Christian Unity*

> The ecumenical commitment of the Catholic Church based on the doctrinal principles of the Second Vatican Council.

II. *Organization in the Catholic Church at the Service of Christian Unity*

> Persons and structures involved in promoting ecumenism at all levels, and the norms that direct their activity.

III. *Ecumenical Formation in the Catholic Church*

> Categories of people to be formed, those responsible for formation; the aim and methods of formation; its doctrinal and practical aspects.

IV. *Communion in Life and Spiritual Activity Among the Baptized*

> The communion that exists with other Christians on the basis of the sacramental bond of Baptism, and the norms for sharing in prayer and other spiritual activities, including in particular cases sacramental sharing.

V. *Ecumenical Cooperation, Dialogue and Common Witness*

> Principles, different forms and norms for cooperation between Christians with a view to dialogue and common witness in the world.

8. Thus, in a time of increasingly marked secularization, which calls Christians to common action in their hope for the Kingdom of God, the norms that regulate relations between Catholics and other Christians and the different forms of collaboration they practice are laid down, so that the promotion of the unity desired by Christ may be sought in a balanced and consistent way, in the line of, and according to the principles established by the Second Vatican Council.

I

THE SEARCH FOR CHRISTIAN UNITY

9. The ecumenical movement seeks to be a response to the gift of God's grace which calls all Christians to faith in the mystery of the Church according to the design of God who wishes to bring humanity to salvation and unity in Christ through the Holy Spirit. This movement calls them to the hope that the prayer of Jesus "that they all may be one" will be fully realized.[9] It calls them to that charity which is the new commandment of Christ and the gift by which the Holy Spirit unites all believers. The Second Vatican Council clearly asked Catholics to reach out in love to all other Christians with a charity that desires and works actively to overcome in truth whatever divides them from one another. For the Council, Catholics are to act in hope and in prayer to promote Christian unity. They will be prompted and instructed by their faith in the mystery of the Church, and their ecumenical activity will be inspired and guided by a true understanding of the Church as "a sacrament or instrumental sign of intimate union with God, and of unity of the whole human race".[10]

10. The teaching of the Church on ecumenism, as well as the encouragement to hope and the invitation to love find their official expression in the documents of the Second Vatican Council and especially in *Lumen Gentium* and *Unitatis Redintegratio*. Subsequent documents about ecumenical activity in the Church, including the Ecumenical Directory (1967-1970) build on the theological, spiritual and pastoral principles stated in the conciliar documents. They have explored more fully some topics indicated in the conciliar documents, developed theological terminology and provided more detailed norms of action, all based, however, on the teaching of the Council itself. All of this furnishes a body of teachings which will be presented in outline in this chapter. These teachings constitute the base of this Directory.

---

[9] *John* 17:21; cf. *Eph* 4:4.
[10] Dogmatic Constitution *Lumen Gentium* (LG), n. 1.

The Church and its Unity in the Plan of God

11.   The Council situates the mystery of the Church within the mystery of God's wisdom and goodness which draws the whole human family and indeed the whole of creation into unity with himself.[11] To this end, God sent into the world His only Son, who was raised up on the cross, entered into glory and poured out the Holy Spirit through whom he calls and draws into unity of faith, hope and charity the people of the New Covenant which is the Church. In order to establish this holy Church in every place until the end of the ages, Christ entrusted to the college of the Twelve to which he chose Peter as head, the office of teaching, ruling and sanctifying. It is the will of Jesus Christ, that through the faithful preaching of the Gospel, the administration of the sacraments, and through government in love exercised by the apostles and their successors under the action of the Holy Spirit, this people should grow and its communion be made ever more perfect.[12] The Council presents the Church as the New People of God, uniting within itself, in all the richness of their diversity, men and women from all nations, all cultures, endowed with manifold gifts of nature and grace, ministering to one another and recognizing that they are sent into the world for its salvation.[13] They accept the Word of God in faith, are baptized into Christ and confirmed in his pentecostal Spirit, and together they celebrate the sacrament of his body and blood in the Eucharist:

> "It is the Holy Spirit, dwelling in those who believe and pervading and ruling over the entire Church, who brings about that wonderful communion of the faithful and joins them together so intimately in Christ that he is the principle of the Church's unity. By distributing various kinds of spiritual gifts and ministeries, he enriches the Church of Jesus Christ with different functions, 'in order to equip the saints for the work of service, so as to build up the Body of Christ' ".[14]

12.   The People of God in its common life of faith and sacraments is served by ordained ministers: bishops, priests and deacons.[15] Thus united in the three-fold bond of faith, sacramental life and hierarchical ministry, the whole People of God comes to be what the tradition of faith from the New Testament [16] onwards

[11] Cf. *LG* 1-4 and also Conciliar Decree on Ecumenism *Unitatis Redintegratio* (UR), n. 2.
[12] Cf. *UR*, n. 2.
[13] *LG*, nn. 2 and 5.
[14] *UR*, n. 2; cf. *Eph* 4:12.
[15] *LG* Chapter III.
[16] *Acts* 2:42.

has always called koinonia/communion. This is a key concept which inspired the ecclesiology of the Second Vatican Council,[17] and to which recent teaching of the magisterium has given great importance.

The Church as Communion

13. The communion in which Christians believe and for which they hope is, in its deepest reality, their unity with the Father through Christ in the Spirit. Since Pentecost, it has been given and received in the Church, the communion of saints. It is accomplished fully in the glory of heaven, but is already realized in the Church on earth as it journeys towards that fullness. Those who live united in faith, hope and love, in mutual service, in common teaching and sacraments, under the guidance of their pastors [18] are part of that communion which constitutes the Church of God. This communion is realized concretely in the particular Churches, each of which is gathered together around its Bishop. In each of these "the one, holy, catholic and apostolic Church of Christ is truly present and alive".[19] This communion is, by its very nature, universal.

14. Communion between the Churches is maintained and manifested in a special way in the communion between their Bishops. Together they form a college which succeeds the apostolic college. This college has as its head the Bishop of Rome as successor of Peter.[20] Thus the Bishops guarantee that the Churches of which they are the ministers continue the one Church of Christ founded on the faith and ministry of the apostles. They coordinate the spiritual energies and the gifts of the faithful and their associations, towards the building up of the Church and of the full exercise of its mission.

15. Each particular Church, united within itself and in the communion of the one, holy catholic and apostolic Church, is sent forth in the name of Christ and in the power of the Spirit to bring the Gospel of the Kingdom to more and more people, offering to them this communion with God. In accepting it, these persons also enter into communion with all those who have already received it and are constituted with them in an authentic family of God. Through its unity this

---

[17] *Relatio Finalis* of the Extraordinary Synod of Bishops in 1985, "The ecclesiology of communion is the central and fundamental idea of the Council's document" (C,1). Cf. Congregation for the Doctrine of the Faith, *Letter to the Bishops of the Catholic Church on certain aspects of the Church as Communion* (28th May 1992).

[18] Cf. *LG*, n. 14.

[19] Conciliar Decree on the Pastoral Office of Bishops in the Church, *Christus Dominus (CD)*, n. 11.

[20] Cf. *LG*, n. 22.

family bears witness to this communion with God. It is in this mission of the Church that the prayer of Jesus is being fulfilled, for he prayed "May they all be one, Father, may they be one in us, as you are in me and I in you, so that the world may believe it was you who sent me".[21]

16. Communion within the particular Churches and between them is a gift of God. It must be received with joyful thanks and cultivated with care. It is fostered in a special way by those who are called to minister in the Church as pastors. The unity of the Church is realized in the midst of a rich diversity. This diversity in the Church is a dimension of its catholicity. At times the very richness of this diversity can engender tensions within the communion. Yet, despite such tensions, the Spirit continues to work in the Church calling Christians in their diversity to ever deeper unity.

17. Catholics hold the firm conviction that the one Church of Christ subsists in the Catholic Church "which is governed by the successor of Peter and by the Bishops in communion with him".[22] They confess that the entirety of revealed truth, of sacraments, and of ministry that Christ gave for the building up of his Church and the carrying out of its mission is found within the Catholic communion of the Church. Certainly Catholics know that personally they have not made full use of and do not make full use of the means of grace with which the Church is endowed. For all that, Catholics never lose confidence in the Church. Their faith assures them that it remains "the worthy bride of the Lord, ceaselessly renewing herself through the action of the Holy Spirit until, through the cross, she may attain to that light which knows no setting".[23] Therefore, when Catholics use the words *"Churches", "other Churches", "other Churches and ecclesial Communities"* etc., to refer to those who are not in full communion with the Catholic Church, this firm conviction and confession of faith must always be kept in mind.

Divisions among Christians and the Re-establishing of Unity

18. Human folly and human sinfulness however have at times opposed the unifying purpose of the Holy Spirit and weakened that power of love which overcomes the inherent tensions in ecclesial life. From the beginning of the Church certain rifts came into being. Then more serious dissensions appeared

[21] *Jn*, 17:21.
[22] *LG*, n. 8.
[23] *LG*, n. 9.

14

and the Churches in the East found themselves no longer in full communion with the See of Rome or with the Church of the West.[24]

Later in the West more profound divisions caused other ecclesial Communities to come into being. These ruptures had to do with doctrinal or disciplinary questions and even with the nature of the Church.[25] The Decree on Ecumenism of the Second Vatican Council recognizes that some dissensions have come about "for which often enough men of both sides were to blame".[26] Yet however much human culpability has damaged communion, it has never destroyed it. In fact, the fullness of the unity of the Church of Christ has been maintained within the Catholic Church while other Churches and ecclesial Communities, though not in full communion with the Catholic Church, retain in reality a certain communion with it. The Council affirms: "This unity, we believe, subsists in the Catholic Church as something she can never lose, and we hope that it will continue to increase until the end of time".[27] The Council documents refer to those elements that are shared by the Catholic Church and the Eastern Churches [28] on the one hand, and the Catholic Church and other Churches and ecclesial Communities on the other:[29] "The Spirit of Christ has not refrained from using them as means of salvation".[30]

19.   No Christian, however, should be satisfied with these forms of communion. They do not correspond to the will of Christ, and weaken his Church in the exercise of its mission. The grace of God has impelled members of many Churches and ecclesial Communities, especially in the course of this present century, to strive to overcome the divisions inherited from the past and to build anew a communion of love by prayer, by repentance and by asking pardon of each other for sins of disunity past and present, by meeting in practical forms of

---

[24] Cf. *UR*, nn. 3 and 13.

[25] Cf. *UR*, n. 3: "Without doubt, the differences that exist in varying degrees between them (other believers in Christ) and the Catholic Church — whether in doctrine and sometimes in discipline, or concerning the structure of the Church — do indeed create many obstacles, sometimes serious ones, to full ecclesial communion. The ecumenical movement is striving to overcome these obstacles." Such divergences continue to have their influence and sometimes they create new divisions.

[26] *UR*, n. 3.

[27] *UR*, n. 4.

[28] Cf. *UR*, nn. 14-18. Those to whom the term *"Orthodox"* is generally applied are those Eastern Churches which accept the decisions of the Councils of Ephesus and Chalcedon. In recent times, however, it has also been applied, for historical reasons, to those Churches which did not accept the dogmatic formulae of one or other of these Councils (cf. *UR*, n. 13). To avoid confusion, the general term *"Eastern Churches"* will be used throughout this Directory to designate all of those Churches of the various Eastern traditions which are not in full communion with the Church of Rome.

[29] Cf. *UR*, nn. 21-23.

[30] *Ibidem*, n. 3.

cooperation and in theological dialogue. These are the aims and activities of what has come to be called the ecumenical movement.[31]

20.   The Catholic Church solemnly pledged itself to work for Christian unity at the Second Vatican Council. The Decree *Unitatis Redintegratio* explains how the unity that Christ wishes for his Church is brought about "through the faithful preaching of the Gospel by the Apostles and their successors—the Bishops with Peter's successor at their head—through their administering the sacraments, and through their governing in love", and defines this unity as consisting of the "confession of one faith,... the common celebration of divine worship,... the fraternal harmony of the family of God".[32] This unity which of its very nature requires full visible communion of all Christians is the ultimate goal of the ecumenical movement. The Council affirms that this unity by no means requires the sacrifice of the rich diversity of spirituality, discipline, liturgical rites and elaborations of revealed truth that has grown up among Christians in the measure that this diversity remains faithful to the apostolic Tradition.[33]

21.   Since the time of the Second Vatican Council ecumenical activity in the entire Catholic Church has been inspired and guided by various documents and initiatives of the Holy See and, in particular Churches, by documents and initiatives of Bishops, Synods of Eastern Catholic Churches and Episcopal Conferences. Also to be noted is the progress made in different kinds of ecumenical dialogue and in the manifold forms of ecumenical collaboration undertaken. Ecumenism has, in the words of the Synod of Bishops of 1985, "inscribed itself deeply and indelibly in the consciousness of the Church".[34]

Ecumenism in the Life of Christians

22.   The ecumenical movement is a grace of God, given by the Father in answer to the prayer of Jesus [35] and the supplication of the Church inspired by the Holy Spirit.[36] While it is carried out within the general mission of the Church to unite humanity in Christ, its own specific field is the restoration of unity among Christians.[37] Those who are baptized in the name of Christ are, by that very fact,

---

[31] Cf. *ibidem*, n. 4.
[32] *UR*, n. 2; *LG*, n. 14; *CIC*, can. 205; *CCEO*, can. 8.
[33] Cf. *UR*, nn. 4 and 15-16.
[34] *Relatio Finalis* of the Extraordinary Synod of Bishops, 1985, C. 7.
[35] Cf. *Jn* 17:21.
[36] Cf. *Rom* 8:26-27.
[37] Cf. *UR*, n. 5.

called to commit themselves to the search for unity.[38] Baptismal communion tends towards full ecclesial communion. To live our Baptism is to be caught up in Christ's mission of making all things one.

23. Catholics are invited to respond according to the directives of their pastors, in solidarity and gratitude with the efforts that are being made in many Churches and ecclesial Communities, and in the various organizations in which they cooperate, to reestablish the unity of Christians. Where ecumenical work is not being done, or not being done effectively, Catholics will seek to promote it. Where it is being opposed or hampered by sectarian attitudes and activities that lead to even greater divisions among those who confess the name of Christ, they should be patient and persevering. At times, local Ordinaries,[39] Synods of Eastern Catholic Churches [40] and Episcopal Conferences may find it necessary to take special measures to overcome the dangers of *indifferentism* or *proselytism*.[41] This may especially be needed in the case of young Churches. In all their contacts with members of other Churches and ecclesial Communities, Catholics will act with honesty, prudence and knowledge of the issues. This readiness to proceed gradually and with care, not glossing over difficulties, is also a safeguard against succumbing to the temptations of indifferentism and proselytism, which would be a failure of the true ecumenical spirit.

24. Whatever the local situation, if they are to be able to carry out their ecumenical responsibilities, Catholics need to act together and in agreement with their Bishops. Above all they should know their own Church and be able to give an account of its teaching, its discipline and its principles of ecumenism. The more they know these, the better they can present them in discussions with other Christians and give sufficient reason for them. They should also have accurate knowledge of the other Churches and ecclesial Communities with whom they are in contact. Careful note must be taken of the various prerequisites for ecumenical engagement that are set out in the Decree on Ecumenism of the Second Vatican Council.[42]

---

[38] Cf. nn. 92-101 below.

[39] In this Directory, when, the term *Local Ordinary* is used, it also refers to *local hierarchies of Eastern Churches* in accordance with the terminology in CCEO.

[40] The term *Synods of Eastern Catholic Churches* refers to the higher authorities of Eastern Catholic Churches sui juris as found in *CCEO*.

[41] Cf. Conciliar Declaration *Dignitatis Humanae* (DH), n. 4: "In spreading religious belief and in introducing religious practices everybody must at all times avoid any action which seems to suggest coercion or dishonest or unworthy persuasion especially when dealing with the uneducated or the poor". At the same time the Declaration affirms that "religious communities have the further right not to be prevented from publicly teaching and bearing witness to their beliefs by the spoken or written word" (*ibidem*).

[42] Cf. *UR*, nn. 9-12; 16-18.

25. Because ecumenism with all its human and moral requirements is rooted so profoundly in the mysterious working out of the providence of the Father, through the Son and in the Spirit, it reaches into the depths of Christian spirituality. It calls for that "change of heart and holiness of life, along with public and private prayer for the unity of Christians", that the Decree on Ecumenism of the Second Vatican Council calls "spiritual ecumenism", and regards as "the soul of the ecumenical movement".[43] Those who identify deeply with Christ must identify with his prayer, and especially with his prayer for unity; those who live in the Spirit must let themselves be transformed by the love that, for the sake of unity, "bears all things, believes all things, hopes all things, endures all things"; [44] those whose lives are marked by repentance will be especially sensitive to the sinfulness of divisions and will pray for forgiveness and conversion. Those who seek holiness be able to recognize its fruits also outside the visible boundaries of their own Church.[45]

They will be led to know, truly, God as the one who alone is able to gather all into unity because he is the Father of all.

The Different Levels of Ecumenical Activity

26. The opportunities and requirements of ecumenical activity do not present themselves in the same way within the parish, in the diocese, within the ambit of a regional or national organization of dioceses, or at the level of the universal Church. Ecumenism requires the involvement of the People of God within the ecclesial structures and the discipline appropriate to each of these levels.

27. In the diocese, gathered around the Bishop, in the parishes and in the various groups and communities, the unity of Christians is being constructed and shown forth day by day: [46] men and women hear the Word of God in faith, pray, celebrate the sacraments, serve one another, and show forth the Gospel of salvation to those who do not yet believe.

However, when members of the same family belong to different Churches and ecclesial Communities, when Christians cannot receive Communion with their spouse or children, or their friends, the pain of division makes itself felt acutely and the impulse to prayer and ecumenical activity should grow.

[43] *UR*, n. 8.
[44] *1 Cor* 13:7.
[45] Cf. *UR*, n. 3.
[46] Cf *LG*, n. 23; *CD*, n. 11; *CIC*, can. 383, 3 and *CCEO*, can. 192, 2.

18

28.   The fact of bringing together particular Churches, belonging to the Catholic communion, to form part of bodies such as Synods of Eastern Catholic Churches and Episcopal Conferences, manifests the communion that exists between those Churches. These assemblies can greatly facilitate the development of effective ecumenical relations with the Churches and ecclesial Communities in the same area that are not in full communion with us. As well as a common cultural and civic tradition, they share a common ecclesial heritage dating from the time before the divisions occurred. Synods of Eastern Catholic Churches and Episcopal Conferences can deal more representatively with these regional or national factors in ecumenism than may be possible for a particular Church, and so may they be able to establish organizations for building up and coordinating ecumenical resources and efforts within the territory, in such a way as to support the activities of particular Churches and help them to follow a coherent Catholic direction in their ecumenical activities.

29.   It belongs to the College of Bishops and to the Apostolic See to judge in the final instance about the manner of responding to the requirements of full communion.[47] It is at this level that the ecumenical experience of all the particular Churches is gathered and evaluated; necessary resources can be coordinated for the service of communion at the universal level and among all the particular Churches that belong to this communion and work for it; directives are given which serve to guide and regulate ecumenical activities throughout the Church. It is often to this level of the Church that other Churches and ecclesial Communities address themselves when they wish to be in ecumenical relation with the Catholic Church. And it is at this level that ultimate decisions about the restoration of communion must be taken.

Complexity and Diversity of the Ecumenical Situation

30.   The ecumenical movement seeks to be obedient to the Word of God, to the promptings of the Holy Spirit and to the authority of those whose ministry it is to ensure that the Church remains faithful to that apostolic Tradition in which the Word of God and the gifts of the Spirit are received. What is being sought is the communion that is at the heart of the mystery of the Church, and for this reason there is a particular need for the apostolic ministry of Bishops in the area of ecumenical activity. The situations being dealt with in ecumenism are often unprecedented, and vary from place to place and time to time. The initiatives of

---

[47] Cf. *CIC*, can. 755, 1; *CCEO*, cann. 902 and 904, 1.

the faithful in the ecumenical domain are to be encouraged. But there is need for constant and careful discernment by those who have ultimate responsibility for the doctrine and the discipline of the Church.[48] It belongs to them to encourage responsible initiatives and to ensure that they are carried out according to Catholic principles of ecumenism. They must reassure those who may be discouraged by difficulties and moderate the imprudent generosity of those who do not give sufficiently serious consideration to the real difficulties in the way of reunion. The Pontifical Council for Promoting Christian Unity, whose role and responsibility it is to provide direction and advice on ecumenical activity, offers the same service to the whole Church.

31.   The nature of the ecumenical activity undertaken in a particular region will always be influenced by the particular character of the local ecumenical situation. The choice of appropriate ecumenical involvement pertains especially to the Bishop who must take account of the specific responsibilities and challenges that are characteristic for his diocese. It is not possible to review here the variety of situations but a few rather general comments can be made.

32.   In a predominantly Catholic country the ecumenical task will emerge differently from that arising in one which has a high proportion or a majority who are Eastern Christians or Anglicans or Protestants. The task is different again in countries where the majority is non-Christian. The participation in the ecumenical movement by the Catholic Church in countries with a large Catholic majority is crucial if ecumenism is to be a movement that involves the whole Church.

33.   Likewise the ecumenical task will greatly vary depending on whether our Christian partners belong mostly to one or more of the Eastern Churches rather than to the Communities of the Reformation. Each has its own dynamic and its own particular possibilities. There are many other factors, political, social, cultural, geographical and ethnic, which can give distinct shape to the ecumenical task.

34.   The particular local context will always furnish the different characteristics of the ecumenical task. What is important is that, in this common effort, Catholics throughout the world support one another with prayer and mutual encouragement so that the quest for Christian unity may be pursued in its many facets in obedience to the command of Our Lord.

---

[48] Cf. *CIC*, cann. 216 and 212; *CCEO*, cann. 19 and 15.

Sects and New Religious Movements

35.   The religious landscape of our world has evolved considerably in recent decades and in some parts of the world the most noticeable development has been the growth of sects and new religious movements whose desire for peaceful relations with the Catholic Church may be weak or non-existent. In 1986, a report [49] was published jointly by four dicasteries of the Roman Curia which draws attention to the vital distinction that must be made between sects and new religious movements on the one hand and Churches and ecclesial Communities on the other. Further studies are in progress on this question.

36.   The situation in regard to sects and new religious movements is highly complex and differs from one cultural context to another. In some countries sects are growing in a cultural climate that is basically religious. In other places they are flourishing in societies that are increasingly secularized but at the same time credulous and superstitious. Some sects are non-Christian in origin and in self-understanding; others are eclectic; others again identify themselves as Christian and may have broken away from Christian Communities or else have links with Christianity. Clearly it is especially up to the Bishop, the Synod of Eastern Catholic Churches or the Episcopal Conference to discern how best to respond to the challenge posed by sects in a given area. But it must be stressed that the principles for spiritual sharing or practical cooperation outlined in this Directory only apply to the Churches and ecclesial Communities with which the Catholic Church has established ecumenical relations. As will be clear to the reader of this Directory, the only basis for such sharing and cooperation is the recognition on both sides of a certain, though imperfect, communion already existing. Openness and mutual respect are the logical consequences of such recognition.

---

[49]   Cf. *Sects or New Religious Movements: A Pastoral Challenge;* an interim Report based on the responses (about 75) and the documentation received up until the 30th of October, 1985 from regional or national Episcopal Conferences, SPCU, *IS* 1986, n. 61, pp. 144-154.

II

THE ORGANIZATION IN THE CATHOLIC CHURCH
OF THE SERVICE OF CHRISTIAN UNITY

Introduction

37. Through its particular Churches, the Catholic Church is present in many localities and regions in which it lives together with other Churches and ecclesial Communities. Such regions have their distinctive spiritual, ethnic, political and cultural characteristics. In many cases one finds in these regions the highest religious authority of other Churches and ecclesial Communities: these regions often correspond to the territory of a Synod of Eastern Catholic Churches or of an Episcopal Conference.

38. Therefore, a Catholic particular Church, or several particular Churches, acting closely together may find themselves in a very favourable position to make contact with other Churches and ecclesial Communities at this level. They may be able to establish with them fruitful ecumenical relations which contribute to the wider ecumenical movement.[50]

39. The Second Vatican Council specifically entrusted the ecumenical task "to the Bishops everywhere in the world for their diligent promotion and prudent guidance".[51] This directive, which has already been acted upon often by individual Bishops, Synods of Eastern Catholic Churches and Episcopal Conferences, has been incorporated into the Canon Law of the Latin Church, canon 755, which states:

§ 1. It is within the special competence of the entire college of Bishops and of the Apostolic See to promote and direct the participation of Catholics in the ecumenical movement, whose purpose is the restoration

---

[50] Cf. nn. 166-171 below.
[51] UR, n. 4.

of unity among all Christians, which the Church is bound by the will of Christ to promote.

§ 2. It is likewise within the competence of Bishops and, in accord with the norms of law, of Conferences of Bishops to promote the same unity and to issue practical norms for the needs and opportunities presented by diverse circumstances in light of the prescriptions of the supreme Church authority.

For the Eastern Catholic Churches the *CCEO,* cann. 902-904, § 1 affirms:

Can. 902: Since concern for the restoration of the unity of all Christians belongs to the entire Church, all Christian faithful, especially pastors of the Church, shall pray for that fullness of unity desired by the Lord and work zealously participating in the ecumenical work brought about by grace of the Holy Spirit.

Can. 903: The Eastern Catholic Churches have a special duty of fostering unity among all Eastern Churches, first of all through prayers, by the example of life, by the religious fidelity to the ancient traditions of the Eastern Churches, by better knowledge of each other, and by collaboration and brotherly respect in practice and spirit.

Can. 904: 1. The undertakings of the ecumenical movement in every Church *sui iuris* are to be diligently encouraged by special norms of particular law, while the Apostolic Roman See directs the movement for the universal Church.

40.   In the light of this special competence for promoting and guiding ecumenical work, it is the responsibility of the individual diocesan Bishop, or of Synods of Eastern Catholic Churches or of Episcopal Conferences to establish norms according to which the persons or commissions described below are to carry out the activities ascribed to them and to oversee the implementation of these norms. Furthermore, care should be taken that those to whom these ecumenical responsibilities are to be assigned have a proper knowledge of the Catholic principles of ecumenism and are seriously prepared for their task.

The Diocesan Ecumenical Officer

41.   In the dioceses, the Bishop should appoint a competent person as diocesan officer for ecumenical questions. He/she will serve as the animator of the diocesan ecumenical Commission and coordinate the Commission's activities as indicated below in n. 44 (or carry them out if such a Commission does not exist). As a close collaborator of the Bishop and with suitable assistance, this person will encourage various initiatives in the diocese for prayer for Christian unity, will work to see that ecumenical attitudes influence the activities of the diocese, identify special needs and keep the diocese informed about these. This officer is also responsible for representing the Catholic community in its relations with the other Churches and ecclesial Communities and their leaders and will facilitate contacts between the latter and the local Bishop, clergy and laity on various levels. He/she will serve as counselor on ecumenical issues for the Bishop and other offices of the diocese and will facilitate the sharing of ecumenical experiences and initiatives with pastors and diocesan organizations. This officer will see to the maintenance of contacts with officers or commissions of other dioceses. Even in areas where Catholics are in majority, or in those dioceses with limited personnel or resources, it is recommended that such a diocesan officer be appointed to carry out the activities mentioned above in so far as these are possible or appropriate.

The Diocesan Ecumenical Commission or Secretariat

42. In addition to the diocesan officer for ecumenical questions, the diocesan Bishop should set up a council, commission or secretariat charged with putting into practice any directives or orientations he may give and, in general, with promoting ecumenical activity in the diocese.[52] Where circumstances call for it, several dioceses grouped together may form such a commission or secretariat.

43. The commission or secretariat should reflect the totality of the diocese and generally include among its members clergy, religious men and women and lay people of various competencies, and especially those with particular ecumenical expertise. It is desirable that representatives of the presbyterial council, the pastoral council, diocesan and regional seminaries be included among the members of the commission or secretariat.

This commission should cooperate with such institutions or ecumenical initiatives as already exist, or are to be set up, making use of their help where the occasion presents itself. It should be ready to support the ecumenical officer and to be available to other diocesan work and individual initiatives for mutual exchange of information and ideas. Of particular concern should be contacts with parishes and parish organizations, with the apostolic initiatives being conducted by members of institutes of consecrated life and societies of apostolic life, and with movements and associations of lay people.

---

[52] Cf. *CCEO*, can. 904, 1; *CIC*, can. 755, 2.

44. Besides the other functions already assigned to it, the commission should:

a) put into practice the decisions of the diocesan Bishop for implementing the teaching and directives of the Second Vatican Council on ecumenism, as well as those of the post-conciliar documents emanating from the Holy See, Synods of Eastern Catholic Churches and Episcopal Conferences;

b) maintain relations with the territorial ecumenical commission (cf. below), adapting the latter's recommendations and advice to local conditions. When circumstances suggest, information about experiences and their results as well as other useful information should be sent to the Pontifical Council for Promoting Christian Unity;

c) foster spiritual ecumenism according to the principles given in the conciliar Decree on Ecumenism and in other sections of this Directory about public and private prayer for the unity of Christians;

d) offer help and encouragement by such means as workshops and seminars for the ecumenical formation of both clergy and laity, for the appropriate realization of an ecumenical dimension to all aspects of life, and giving special attention as to how seminary students are prepared for the ecumenical dimension of preaching, catechetics and other forms of teaching, and pastoral activity (e.g., pastoral care in mixed marriages) etc.;

e) promote friendliness and charity between Catholics and other Christians with whom full ecclesial communion does not yet exist according to the suggestions and guidelines given below (especially nn. 205-218);

f) initiate and guide conversations and consultations with them, bearing in mind the adaptation to be observed in accordance with the diversity of the participants and subjects of dialogue; [53]

g) propose experts to undertake dialogue on the diocesan level with other Churches and ecclesial Communities;

h) promote, in collaboration with other diocesan bodies and with other Christians joint witness to Christian faith, to the extent that this is possible, as well as cooperation in such areas as education, public and private morality, social justice, matters connected with culture, learning and the arts; [54]

---

[53] Cf. *UR,* nn. 9 and 11 and *Reflections and Suggestions Concerning Ecumenical Dialogue,* op.cit.

[54] Cf. *UR,* n. 12; Conciliar Decree on the Church's Missionary Activity *Ad Gentes* (AG), n. 12, and *Ecumenical Collaboration at the Regional, National and Local Levels,* op. cit., n. 3.

i) propose to the Bishops the exchange of observers and guests on the occasion of important conferences, synods, installation of religious leaders and other similar occasions.

45.   Within the dioceses, parishes should be encouraged to participate in ecumenical initiatives on their own level and, where possible to set up groups which are responsible to carry out these activities (cf. below, n. 67); they should remain in close contact with the diocesan authorities, exchanging information and experience with them and with other parishes and other groups.

The Ecumenical Commission of Synods of Eastern Catholic Churches and Episcopal Conferences

46.   Each Synod of the Eastern Catholic Churches and each Episcopal Conference, in accordance with its own procedures, should establish an episcopal commission for ecumenism, assisted by experts, both men and women, chosen from among the clergy, religious and laity. If possible, the commission should be assisted by a permanent secretariat. This commission, whose method of work will be determined by the statutes of the synod or conference, should have a mandate to give guidance in ecumenical affairs and determine concrete ways of acting in accordance with existing church legislation, directives and legitimate customs and the concrete possibilities of a given region. It should take into account the circumstances of place and persons of the territory with whom they are concerned, as well as the concerns of the universal Church. Where the size of an Episcopal Conference does not permit the establishment of a commission of Bishops, at least one Bishop should be named to assume responsibility for the ecumenical tasks indicated in n. 47.

47.   The functions of this commission will include those listed under n. 44 above, insofar as they enter into the competence of the Synods of Eastern Catholic Churches or Episcopal Conferences. In addition, it should carry out other tasks, of which some examples are given here:

a) putting into practice the norms and instructions issued by the Holy See in these matters;

b) giving advice and assistance to Bishops who are setting up an ecumenical commission in their dioceses, and encouraging cooperation among the diocesan ecumenical officers and commissions themselves by sponsoring, for example, periodic gatherings of officers and representatives from diocesan commissions;

c) encouraging and, where indicated, assisting the other commissions of the Episcopal Conferences and Synods of Eastern Catholic Churches in taking account of the ecumenical dimension of the latter's work, public statements, etc.;

d) promoting cooperation among Christians, for example by giving spiritual and material help, where possible, to both existing ecumenical institutions and to ecumenical initiatives to be fostered in the field of instruction and research or in that of pastoral care and the deepening of Christian life according to the principles set out in the conciliar Decree on Ecumenism, nn. 9-12;

e) establishing consultations and dialogue with the church leaders and with Councils of Churches which exist on a national or territorial (as distinct from the diocesan) level and providing adequate structures for these dialogues;

f) appointing those experts who, by an official mandate of the Church, will participate in the consultations and dialogues with experts of the various Churches and ecclesial Communities, and with the organizations mentioned above;

g) maintaining relations and active cooperation with the ecumenical structures established by institutes of consecrated life and societies of apostolic life and with those of other Catholic organizations within the territory;

h) organizing the exchange of observers and guests on the occasion of important ecclesial convocations and similar events at the national or territorial levels;

i) informing the Bishops of the Conference and of the Synods about the developments of the dialogues taking place in the territory; sharing this information with the Pontifical Council for Promoting Christian Unity in Rome, so that mutual exchange of advice, experience and the results of dialogue can promote other dialogues on different levels of the life of the Church;

j) in general, maintaining relations in ecumenical matters between the Synods of the Eastern Catholic Churches or Episcopal Conferences and the Pontifical Council for Promoting Christian Unity in Rome, as well as with the ecumenical commissions of other territorial Conferences.

Ecumenical Structures within other Ecclesial Contexts

48. Supranational bodies which exist in various forms for assuring cooperation and assistance among Episcopal Conferences should also establish some structures for ensuring the ecumenical dimension of their work. The scope of their activities and the form these may take will be determined by the statutes and procedures of each of their bodies and the concrete possibilities of the territory.

49. Within the Catholic Church, certain communities and organizations exist which have a specific place in contributing to the apostolic life of the Church. While they do not immediately form part of the ecumenical structures described above, their work very frequently has an important ecumenical dimension which should be organized into adequate structures according to the fundamental purposes of the organization. Among these communities and organizations are found institutes of consecrated life, societies of apostolic life and various organizations of Catholic faithful.

Institutes of Consecrated Life and Societies of Apostolic Life

50. While the concern for restoring Christian unity involves the whole Church, clergy and laity alike,[55] religious orders and congregations and societies of apostolic life, by the very nature of their particular commitments in the Church and the contexts in which they live out these commitments, have significant opportunities of fostering ecumenical thought and action. In accordance with their particular charisms and constitutions—some of which antedate the divisions among Christians—and in the light of the spirit and aims of their institutes, they are encouraged to put into practice, within the concrete possibilities and limits of their rules of life, the following attitudes and activities:

> *a)* to foster an awareness of the ecumenical importance of their particular forms of life in as much as conversion of heart, personal holiness, public and private prayer and disinterested service to the Church and the world are at the heart of the ecumenical movement;

> *b)* to contribute to an understanding of the ecumenical dimensions of the vocation of all Christians to holiness of life by offering occasions for developing spiritual formation, contemplation, adoration and praise of God and service to one's neighbour;

[55] Cf. *UR,* n. 5.

c) taking account of the circumstances of place and persons, to organise meetings among Christians of various Churches and ecclesial Communities for liturgical prayer, for recollection and spiritual exercises, and for a more profound understanding of Christian spiritual traditions;

d) to maintain relations with monasteries or communities of common life in other Christian Communions for an exchange of spiritual and intellectual resources, and experiences in apostolic life, since the growth of the religious charisms in these Communions can be a positive factor for the whole of the ecumenical movement. This can provide a fruitful spiritual emulation;

e) to conduct their many varied educational institutions with a view to ecumenical activity in accordance with the principles presented further on in this Directory;

f) to collaborate with other Christians in the areas of common work for social justice, economic development, progress in health and education, the safeguarding of creation, and for peace and reconciliation among nations and communities;

g) insofar as religious conditions permit, ecumenical action should be encouraged, so that, "while avoiding every form of indifferentism, or confusion and also senseless rivalry, Catholics might collaborate with their separated brethren, insofar as it is possible, by a common profession before the nations of faith in God and in Jesus Christ, and by a common, fraternal effort in social, cultural, technical and religious matters, in accordance with the Decree on Ecumenism. Let them cooperate, especially, because of Christ their common Lord. May his Name unite them!".[56]

In carrying out these activities, they will observe the norms for ecumenical work which have been established by the diocesan Bishop, the Synods of Eastern Catholic Churches or Episcopal Conferences as an element of their cooperation in the total apostolate of a given territory. They will maintain close contacts with the various dioceses or national ecumenical commissions and, where indicated, with the Pontifical Council for Promoting Christian Unity.

51. To assist this ecumenical activity, it is very opportune that the various institutes of consecrated life and societies of apostolic life establish, on the level of their central authorities, a delegate or a commission charged with promoting and

---

[56] Cf. *AG,* n. 15; see also *ibidem,* nn. 5 and 29; cf. *EN,* nn. 23, 28, 77; see also below, nn. 205-209.

assisting their ecumenical engagement. The function of these delegates or commissions will be to encourage the ecumenical formation of all the members, aid the specific ecumenical formation of those who have particular offices and act as advisors for ecumenical affairs to the various general and local authorities of the institutes and societies, especially for initiating or carrying forward the activities described above (n. 50).

Organizations of Faithful

52. Organizations of Catholic faithful in a particular territory or nation, as well as those of an international character having as their objectives, e.g., spiritual renewal, action for peace and social justice, education at various levels, economic aid to countries and institutions, etc., should develop the ecumenical aspects of their activities. They should see that the ecumenical dimensions of their work be given adequate attention and expression even, if necessary, in their statutes and structures. In carrying out their ecumenical activities, they should remain in contact with territorial and local ecumenical commissions and, where circumstances indicate it, with the Pontifical Council for Promoting Christian Unity for fruitful exchanges of experiences and advice.

The Pontifical Council for Promoting Christian Unity

53. At the level of the universal Church, the Pontifical Council for Promoting Christian Unity, a department of the Roman Curia, has the competence and the task of promoting full communion among all Christians. The Constitution *Pastor Bonus* (cf. n. 6 above) states that it promotes, on the one hand, the ecumenical spirit and action within the Catholic Church and, on the other hand, it cultivates relations with the other Churches and ecclesial Communities.

> *a)* The Pontifical Council is concerned with the proper interpretation of the principles of ecumenism, and the means of putting them into effect; it implements the decisions of the Second Vatican Council with regard to ecumenism; it encourages and assists national or international groups which promote the unity of Christians and helps coordinate their work.

> *b)* It organizes official dialogues with other Churches and ecclesial Communities on the international level; it delegates Catholic observers on the international level; it delegates Catholic observers to conferences

or meetings of these bodies or of other ecumenical organizations and invites observers from them to meetings of the Catholic Church, whenever this is judged opportune.

54.   To fulfil these functions, the Pontifical Council for Promoting Christian Unity at times issues directives and guidelines applicable to the entire Catholic Church. Furthermore, it maintains contacts with the Synods of Eastern Catholic Churches and Episcopal Conferences, with their ecumenical commissions, and with the Bishops and organizations within the Catholic Church. The coordination of the ecumenical activities of the entire Catholic Church requires that these contacts be reciprocal. It is therefore appropriate that the Council be informed of important initiatives taken at various levels of the life of the Church. This is necessary, in particular, when these initiatives have international implications such as when important dialogues are organized at a national or territorial level with other Churches and ecclesial Communities. The mutual exchange of information and advice will benefit ecumenical activities at the international level as well as those on every other level of the Church's life. Whatever facilitates a growth of harmony and of coherent ecumenical engagement also reinforces communion within the Catholic Church.

III

ECUMENICAL FORMATION
IN THE CATHOLIC CHURCH

The Necessity and Purpose of Ecumenical Formation

55. "Concern for restoring unity pertains to the whole Church, faithful and clergy alike. It extends to everyone, according to the potential of each, whether it be exercised in daily Christian living or in theological and historical studies".[57] Bearing in mind the nature of the Catholic Church, Catholics will find, if they follow faithfully the indications of the Second Vatican Council, the means of contributing to the ecumenical formation, both of individuals and of the whole community to which they belong. Thus the unity of all in Christ will be the result of a common growth and maturing. For God's call to interior conversion[58] and renewal[59] in the Church, so fundamental to the quest for unity, excludes no one.

For that reason, all the faithful are called upon to make a personal commitment toward promoting increasing communion with other Christians. But there is a particular contribution that can be made to this by those members of the People of God who are engaged in formation—such as heads and staffs of colleges of higher and specialized education. Those who do pastoral work, and especially parish priests and other ordained ministers, also have their role to play in this matter. It is the responsibility of each Bishop, of Synods of Eastern Catholic Churches and of Episcopal Conferences to issue general directives relating to ecumenical formation.

Adaptation of Formation to the Concrete Situation of Persons

56. Ecumenism calls for renewal of attitudes and for flexibility of methods in the search for unity. Account must also be taken of the variety of persons, func-

---

[57] UR, n. 5.
[58] Cf. *ibidem*, n. 7.
[59] *Ibidem*, n. 6.

tions, situations and even of the specific character of the particular Churches, and the communities engaged with them, in the search for unity. Consequently, ecumenical formation requires a pedagogy that is adapted to the concrete situation of the life of persons and groups, and which respects the need for gradualness in an effort of continual renewal and of change in attitudes.

57. Not only teachers, but all those who are involved in pastoral work will be progressively formed in accordance with the following principal orientations:

a) Knowledge of Scripture and doctrinal formation are necessary from the outset, together with knowledge of the history and of the ecumenical situation in the country where one lives.

b) Knowledge of the history of divisions and of efforts at reconciliation, as well as the doctrinal positions of other Churches and ecclesial Communities will make it possible to analyse problems in their socio-cultural context and to discern in expressions of faith what is legitimate diversity and what constitutes divergence that is incompatible with Catholic faith.

c) This perspective will take account of the results and clarifications coming from theological dialogues and scientific studies. It is even desirable that Christians should write together the history of their divisions and of their efforts in the search for unity.

d) In this way the danger of subjective interpretations can be avoided, both in the presentation of the Catholic faith and also in Catholic understanding of the faith and of the life of other Churches and ecclesial Communities.

e) In so far as it progresses well, ecumenical formation makes concern for the unity of the Catholic Church and concern for communion with other Churches and ecclesial Communities inseparable.

f) It is implicit in the concern for this unity and this communion that Catholics should be concerned to deepen relations both with Eastern Christians and Christians in communities issuing from the Reformation.

g) The method of teaching should allow for the necessity of progressing gradually. Such a method makes it possible to distinguish and distribute the questions to be studied and their respective contents in the various phases of doctrinal formation, taking account also of the ecumenical experience of the person concerned.

34

Thus, all those engaged in pastoral work will be faithful to the holy and living Tradition which is a source of initiative within the Church. They should be able to evaluate and welcome truth wherever it is found. "All truth, by whomsoever it is spoken, is of the Holy Spirit".[60]

A. FORMATION OF ALL THE FAITHFUL

58. The concern for unity is fundamental to the understanding of the Church. The objective of ecumenical formation is that all Christians be animated by the ecumenical spirit, whatever their particular mission and task in the world and in society.

In the life of the faithful, imbued with the Spirit of Christ, the gift prayed for by Christ before his passion, the "grace of unity", is of primary importance. This unity is first of all unity with Christ in a single movement of charity extending both towards the Father and towards the neighbour. Secondly, it is a profound and active communion of the individual faithful with the universal Church within the particular Church to which he or she belongs.[61] And thirdly it is the fullness of visible unity which is sought with Christians of other Churches and ecclesial Communities.

The Means of Formation

59. *Hearing and studying the Word of God.* The Catholic Church has always considered Scriptures, together with Tradition, "as the supreme rule of faith"; they are for its children "the food of the soul, the pure and perennial source of spiritual life".[62] Our brothers and sisters of other Churches and ecclesial Communities have a deep love and reverence for the Holy Scriptures. This occasions their constant and deep study of the sacred books.[63] The Word of God, then, being one and the same for all Christians, will progressively strengthen the path towards unity insofar as it is approached with religious attention and loving study.

60. *Preaching.* Particular care must be taken with preaching, whether within or outside of liturgical worship as such. As Paul VI says: "As evangelizers, we

---

[60] Ambrosiaster, *PL* 17, 245.
[61] Cf. *CIC,* can. 209, 1; *CCEO,* can. 12, 1.
[62] Dogmatic Constitution on Divine Revelation *Dei Verbum* (DV), n. 21.
[63] Cf. *UR,* n. 21.

must offer Christ's faithful not the image of a people divided and separated by unedifying quarrels, but the image of people who are mature in faith and capable of finding a meeting-point beyond the real tensions, thanks to a shared, sincere and disinterested search for truth".[64] The different parts of the liturgical year offer favourable opportunities for developing the themes of Christian unity, and for stimulating study, reflection and prayer.

Preaching should concern itself with revealing the mystery of the unity of the Church, and as far as possible promoting visibly the unity of Christians. In preaching, any improper use of Scripture must be avoided.

61. _Catechesis._ Catechesis is not only the teaching of doctrine, but initiation into the Christian life as a whole, with full participation in the sacraments of the Church. But, as shown in Pope John Paul II's Apostolic Exhortation _Catechesi Tradendae_ (nn. 32-33), this teaching can help to form a genuine ecumenical attitude, by observing the following directives:

> _a)_ First, it should expound clearly, with charity and with due firmness the whole doctrine of the Catholic Church respecting in a particular way the order of the hierarchy of truths [65] and avoiding expressions and ways of presenting doctrine which would be an obstacle to dialogue.

> _b)_ When speaking of other Churches and ecclesial Communities, it is important to present their teaching correctly and honestly. Among those elements by which the Church itself is built up and given life, some—even many and very valuable ones—are to be found outside the visible limits of the Catholic Church.[66] The Spirit of Christ therefore does not refuse to use these communities as means of salvation. Doing this also puts in relief the truths of faith held in common by various Christian confessions. This will help Catholics both to deepen their own faith and to know and esteem other Christians, thus making easier the search in common for the path of full unity in the whole truth.[67]

> _c)_ Catechesis will have an ecumenical dimension if it arouses and nourishes a true desire for unity and still more if it fosters real effort, including efforts in humility to purify ourselves, so as to remove obstacles on the way, not by facile doctrinal omissions and concessions, but by aim-

---

[64] _EN_, n. 77.
[65] Cf. _UR_, n. 11; _AG_, n. 15. For these considerations, cf. _General Catechetical Directory_, nn. 27, 43, and cf. below nn. 75 and 176.
[66] Cf. _UR_, nn. 3-4.
[67] Cf. _CT_, n. 3 and _CCEO_, can. 625.

ing at that perfect unity which the Lord wills and by using the means that He wills.[68]

d) Catechesis will, moreover, have this ecumenical dimension if it sets out to prepare children and young people as well as adults to live in contact with other Christians, maturing as Catholics while growing in respect for the faith of others.[69]

e) It can do this by discerning the possibilities offered by the distinction between the truths of faith and their modes of expression; [70] by mutual striving to understand and esteem what is good in each other's theological traditions; by making clear that dialogue has created new relationships which, if they are well understood, can lead to collaboration and peace.[71]

f) The Apostolic Exhortation *Catechesi Tradendae* should be a point of reference in the elaboration of new catechisms which are prepared in local Churches under the authority of the Bishops.

62. *Liturgy.* Being "the primary and indispensable source from which the faithful are to derive the true Christian spirit",[72] liturgy makes an important contribution to the unity of all who believe in Christ; it is a celebration and an agent of unity; where it is fully understood and everybody fully participates in it, "it is (thus) the outstanding means by which the faithful can express in their lives, and manifest to others, the mystery of Christ and the real nature of the true Church".[73]

a) Since the holy Eucharist is "the wonderful sacrament... by which the unity of the Church is both signified and brought about",[74] it is very important to see that it is celebrated well so that the faithful can participate in it, because "by offering the Immaculate Victim not only through the hands of the priest but also with him, they should learn to offer themselves too. Through Christ the Mediator they should be drawn day by day into ever closer union with God and with each other, so that finally God may be all in all".[75]

---

[68] Cf. *CT*, n. 32.
[69] Cf. *ibidem.*
[70] Cf. *UR*, n. 6 and Pastoral Constitution on the Church in the Modern World *Gaudium et Spes* (GS), n. 62.
[71] Concerning ecumenical collaboration in the field of catechesis, see *CT*, n. 33 and also nn. 188-190 below.
[72] See Constitution on the Sacred Liturgy *Sacrosanctum Concilium* (SC), n. 14.
[73] *Ibidem,* n. 2.
[74] *UR*, n. 2.
[75] *SC*, n. 48.

b) It would be good to foster fidelity to prayer for Christian unity, according to the indications of this Directory, whether at the times the liturgy indicates—as, for example, in celebrations of the Word or else at Eastern celebrations known as "Litia" and "Moleben"—or especially during Mass—in the prayer for the faithful or the "Ectenie" litanies, or also in celebration of the votive Mass for Unity of the Church, with the help of the appropriate formularies.

An efficacious formation can also be obtained by intensifying prayer for unity at special times, such as Unity Week (18-25 January) or the week between Ascension and Pentecost, so that the Holy Spirit may confirm the Church in its unity and in the apostolicity of its universal saving mission.

63. *The spiritual life.* In the ecumenical movement it is necessary to give priority to conversion of heart, spiritual life and its renewal. "This change of heart and holiness of life, along with public and private prayer for the unity of Christians, should be regarded as the soul of the whole ecumenical movement, and can rightly be called 'spiritual ecumenism' ".[76] Individual Christians, therefore, insofar as they live a genuine spiritual life with Christ the Saviour as its centre and the glory of God the Father as its goal, can always and everywhere share deeply in the ecumenical movement, witnessing to the Gospel of Christ with their lives.[77]

> *a)* Catholics should also give value to certain elements and goods, sources of spiritual life, which are found in other Churches and ecclesial Communities, and which belong to the one Church of Christ: Holy Scripture, the sacraments and other sacred actions, faith, hope, charity and other gifts of the Spirit.[78] These goods have borne fruit for example in the mystical tradition of the Christian East and the spiritual treasures of the monastic life, in the worship and piety of Anglicans, in the evangelical prayer and the diverse forms of Protestant spirituality.

> *b)* This appreciation should not remain merely theoretical; in suitable particular conditions, it should be completed by the practical knowledge of other traditions of spirituality. Therefore, sharing prayer and participating in some form of public worship or in devotional acts of other Christians can have a formative value when in accord with existing directives.[79]

---

[76] *UR,* n. 8.
[77] Cf. *ibidem,* n. 7.
[78] Cf. *LG,* n. 15 and *UR,* n. 3.
[79] Cf. nn. 102-142 below.

64. *Other initiatives.* Collaboration in social and charitable initiatives in contexts such as schools, hospitals and prisons, has a proven formational value. So too has work for peace in the world or in particular regions where it is threatened, and for human rights and religious liberty.[80]

These activities, properly directed, can show the efficacy of the social application of the Gospel and the practical force of ecumenical sensitivity in various places. Periodic reflection on the Christian basis of such activities, testing their quality and their fruitfulness, while correcting their defects, will also be educative and constructive.

Suitable Settings for Formation

65. These are the places where human and Christian maturity, the sense of companionship and communion, grow step by step. Of particular importance in this connection are family, parish, school, different groups, associations and ecclesial movements.

66. *The family,* called the "domestic church" by the Second Vatican Council,[81] is the primary place in which unity will be fashioned or weakened each day through the encounter of persons, who, though different in many ways, accept each other in a communion of love. It is also there that care must be taken not to entertain prejudices, but on the contrary to search for the truth in all things.

> *a)* Awareness of its Christian identity and mission makes the family ready to be a community for others, a community not only open to the Church but also to human society, ready for dialogue and social involvement. Like the Church, it should be a setting in which the Gospel is transmitted and which radiates the Gospel; indeed *Lumen Gentium* states that in the domestic church "parents should by their words and example be the first preachers of the faith to their children" (n. 11).

> *b)* Mixed marriage families have the duty to proclaim Christ with the fullness implied in a common baptism, they have too the delicate task of making themselves builders of unity.[82] "Their common baptism and the dynamism of grace provide the spouses in these marriages with the

---

[80] Cf. nn. 161-218 below.
[81] *LG*, n. 11.
[82] Cf. *EN*, n. 71; see also nn. 143-160 below.

basis and motivation for expressing their unity in the sphere of moral and spiritual values".[83]

67.   *The parish,* as an ecclesial unity gathered around the Eucharist, should be, and proclaim itself to be the place of authentic ecumenical witness. Thus a great task for the parish is to educate its members in the ecumenical spirit. This calls for care with the content and form of preaching, especially of the homily, and with catechesis. It calls too for a pastoral programme which involves someone charged with promoting and planning ecumenical activity, working in close harmony with the parish priest; this will help in the various forms of collaboration with the corresponding parishes of other Christians. Finally it demands that the parish be not torn apart by internal polemics, ideological polarization or mutual recrimination between Christians, but that everyone, according to his or her own spirit and calling, serve the truth in love.[84]

68.   *The school,* of every kind and grade, should give an ecumenical dimension to its religious teaching, and should aim in its own way to train hearts and minds in human and religious values, educating for dialogue, for peace and for personal relationships.[85]

> *a)* The spirit of charity, of respect, and of dialogue demands the elimination of language and prejudices which distort the image of other Christians. This holds especially for Catholic schools where the young must grow in faith, in prayer, in resolve to put into practice the Christian Gospel of unity. They should be taught genuine ecumenism, according to the doctrine of the Catholic Church.

> *b)* Where possible, in collaboration with other teachers, different subjects, e.g. history and art, should be treated in a way that underlines the ecumenical problems in a spirit of dialogue and unity. To this end it is also desirable that teachers be correctly and adequately informed about the origins, history and doctrines of other Churches and ecclesial Communities especially those that exist in their region.

69.   *Groups, associations, ecclesial movements.* Christian life, notably the life of particular Churches has been enriched throughout history by a variety of expressions, enterprises and spiritualities, according to the charisms given by the Spirit for the building up of the Church, revealing a clear distinction of tasks in the service of the community.

---

[83] Pope John Paul II, Apostolic Exhortation *Familiaris Consortio* (FC), n. 78.
[84] Cf. *CIC,* can. 529, 2.
[85] Cf. Conciliar Declaration *Gravissimum Educationis* (GE), nn. 6-9.

40

Those involved in such groups, movements and associations should be imbued with a solid ecumenical spirit, in living out their baptismal commitment in the world,[86] whether by seeking Catholic unity through dialogue and communion with similar movements and associations—or the wider communion with other Churches and ecclesial Communities and with the movements and groups inspired by them. These efforts should be carried out on the basis of a sound formation and in the light of Christian wisdom and prudence.

B. FORMATION OF THOSE ENGAGED IN PASTORAL WORK

1. ORDAINED MINISTERS

70. Among the principal duties of every future ordained minister is to shape his own personality, to the extent possible, in such a way as will serve his mission of helping others to meet Christ. In this perspective, the candidate for the ministry needs to develop fully those human qualities which make a person acceptable and credible among people, checking regularly his own language and capacity for dialogue so as to acquire an authentically ecumenical disposition. If this is essential for one who has the office of teacher and shepherd in a particular Church, like the Bishop, or one who as a priest takes care of souls, it is no less important for the deacon, and in a particular way for the permanent deacon, who is called to serve the community of the faithful.

71. In taking initiatives and promoting encounters, the minister must act clearly and with faithfulness to the Church, respecting the authority of others and following the disposition which the pastors of the Church are entitled to make for the ecumenical movement in the universal Church and in the single local Churches, to ensure that collaboration in the building-up of Christian unity shall be free of prejudice and ill-considered initiatives.

a) DOCTRINAL FORMATION

72. Episcopal Conferences should ensure that plans of study give an ecumenical dimension to each subject and provide specifically for the study of ecumenism. They should also ensure that plans of study are in conformity with the indications contained in this Directory.

---

[86] Cf. *LG*, n. 31.

73.   Ecumenical activity "has to be fully and sincerely Catholic, that is, faithful to the truth we have received from the Apostles and the Fathers and consonant with the faith the Catholic Church has always professed".[87]

74.   Students must learn to distinguish between on the one hand revealed truths, which all require the same assent of faith, and on the other hand the manner of stating those truths and theological doctrines.[88] As far as the formulation of revealed truths is concerned, account will be taken of what is said by, among others, the declaration of the Congregation for the Doctrine of the Faith's *Mysterium Ecclesiae*, n. 5: "The truths which the Church intends actually to teach through its dogmatic formularies are, without doubt, distinct from the changing conceptions proper to a given age and can be expressed without them, but it can nonetheless happen that they will be expressed by the magisterium, in terms that bear traces of those conceptions. Account having been taken of these considerations, it must also be said that from the beginning the dogmatic formularies of the magisterium have always been appropriate for communicating revealed truth and that, remaining unchanged, they will always communicate it to those who interpret them properly".[89] Students should therefore learn to make the distinction between the "deposit of faith itself or the truths which are contained in our venerable doctrine",[90] and the way in which these truths are formulated; between the truths to be proclaimed and the various ways of perceiving them and shedding light upon them; between the apostolic Tradition and strictly ecclesiastical traditions, and at the same time they should learn to recognize and respect the permanent value of dogmatic formulations. From the time of their philosophical formation, students should be prepared to appreciate the legitimate diversity in theology which derives from the different methods and language theologians use in penetrating the divine mysteries. From which it follows that different theological formulations are often more complementary than contradictory.

75.   Moreover, the "hierarchy of truths" of Catholic doctrine should always be respected; these truths all demand due assent of faith, yet are not all equally cen-

---

[87] *UR*, n. 24.
[88] Cf. *GS*, n. 62, 2; *UR*, n. 6; Congregation for the Doctrine of the Faith *Mysterium Ecclesiae* (ME), n. 5.
[89] *ME*, n. 5.
[90] *Ecumenical Directory*, *AAS* 1970, n. 74.

tral to the mystery revealed in Jesus Christ, since they vary in their connection with the foundation of the Christian faith.[91]

a–2) *The Ecumenical Dimension of Theological Disciplines in general*

76. Ecumenical openness is a constitutive dimension of the formation of future priests and deacons: "Sacred theology and other branches of knowledge, especially those of an historical nature, must be taught with due regard for the ecumenical point of view, so that they may correspond as exactly as possible with the facts".[92] The ecumenical dimension in theological formation should not be limited to different categories of teaching. Because we are talking about interdisciplinary teaching—and not only "pluridisciplinary"—this will involve cooperation between the professors concerned and reciprocal coordination. In each subject, even in those which are fundamental, the following aspects may be suitably emphasized:

> *a)* the elements of the Christian patrimony of truth and holiness which are common to all Churches and ecclesial Communities, even though these are sometimes presented according to varying theological expressions;

> *b)* the riches of liturgy, spirituality and doctrine proper to each communion, but which can help Christians towards a deeper knowledge of the nature of the Church;

> *c)* points of disagreement on matters of faith and morals which can nonetheless encourage deeper exploration of the Word of God and lead to distinguishing real from apparent contradictions.

a–3) *The Ecumenical Dimension of Individual Theological Disciplines*

77. In every theological discipline an ecumenical approach should bring us to consider the link between the particular subject and the mystery of the unity of the Church. Moreover, the teacher should instil in his students fidelity to the whole authentic Christian Tradition in matters of theology, spirituality and ecclesiastical discipline. When students compare their own patrimony with the riches of the other Christian traditions of East and West, whether in their ancient or modern expression, they will become more deeply conscious of this fullness.[93]

---

[91] Cf. *ME*, n. 4; see also nn. 61a and 176.
[92] *UR*, n. 10; cf. *CIC*, can. 256, 2; *CCEO*, cann. 350, 4 and 352, 3.
[93] Cf. *UR*, nn. 14-17.

78. This comparative study is important in all subjects: in the study of Scripture, which is the common source of faith for all Christians; in the study of the apostolic Tradition in the Fathers of the Church and in other church writers of East and West; of liturgy, where the various forms of divine worship and their doctrinal and spiritual importance are scientifically compared; in dogmatic and moral theology, especially in respect of problems arising from ecumenical dialogue; in church history, where there should be a careful enquiry into the unity of the Church and into the causes of separation; in canon law, which must distinguish clearly between divine law and those ecclesiastical laws which can change with time, culture or local tradition; and finally, in pastoral and missionary training and sociological studies, which must pay attention to the conditions common to all Christians facing the modern world. Thus the fullness of Divine Revelation will be expressed in a better and more complete way, and we will better fulfil the mission for the world which Christ entrusted to his Church.

a–4) *A Specific Course in Ecumenism*

79. Even though an ecumenical dimension should permeate all theological formation, it is of particular importance that a course in ecumenism be given at an appropriate point in the first cycle. Such a course should be compulsory. In broad and adaptable terms, it might have the following content:

a) the notions of catholicity, of the visible and organic unity of the Church, of the *oecumene,* ecumenism; from their historical origins to the present meaning from the Catholic viewpoint;

b) the doctrinal basis of ecumenical activity with particular reference to the already existing bonds of communion between Churches and ecclesial Communities; [94]

c) the history of ecumenism, which includes that of the divisions and of the many attempts during the ages to reestablish unity, their achievements and failures, the present state of the search for unity;

d) the purpose and method of ecumenism, the various forms of union and of collaboration, the hope of re-establishing unity, the conditions of unity, the concept of full and perfect unity;

e) the "institutional" aspect and the contemporary life in the various Christian Communities: doctrinal tendencies, the real causes of separa-

---

[94] Cf. *UR,* chap. I.

tions, missionary efforts, spirituality, forms of worship, need for better knowledge of Eastern theology and spirituality; [95]

f) some more specific problems such as shared worship, proselytism and irenicism, religious freedom, mixed marriages, the role of the laity and, in particular, of women in the Church;

g) spiritual ecumenism, especially the significance of prayer for unity and other forms of tending towards the unity prayed for by Christ.

80. Studies might be organized on some plan such as this:

a) it would be good if a general introduction to ecumenism were offered fairly early so that the students could be sensitized, right from the beginning of their theological studies, to the ecumenical dimension of their studies.[96] This introduction would deal with the basic questions in ecumenism;

b) the specific part of the teaching on ecumenism would find its normal place towards the end either of the first cycle of theological studies or of the seminary course, so that the students in gaining a broad knowledge of ecumenism could make a synthesis of this with their theological formation;

c) text books and other aids should be carefully chosen: they should expound with fidelity the teaching of other Christians in history, theology and spirituality so as to permit honest and objective comparisons and to stimulate a further deepening of Catholic doctrine.

81. It would be useful to invite lecturers and experts of other traditions, in the context of the directives on collaboration between Catholic institutions and the centres under the auspices of other Christians.[97] In case of particular problems arising in respect of a specific seminary or institute, it is up to the diocesan Bishop to decide, according to the norms established by the Episcopal Conference and after having ascertained the moral and professional qualities of prospective lecturers from other Churches and ecclesial Communities, which of the initiatives can be pursued under the specific responsibility of the academic authorities. In these cultural exchanges, the continuing Catholic character of the institution in question as well as its right and duty to form its own candidates and to teach Catholic doctrine according to the norms of the Church, should always be ensured.

---

[95] Cf. *ibidem,* chap. III.
[96] Cf. nn. 76-80 above.
[97] Cf. nn. 194-195 below.

b) Ecumenical Experience

82. In the formative period, in order that the approach to ecumenism is not cut off from life but rooted in the living experience of communities, encounters and discussions can usefully be organized with other Christians, at the universal and the local level, while observing the relative norms of the Catholic Church.

Representatives of other communities with a professional and religious preparation and the ecumenical spirit necessary for a sincere and constructive dialogue may be invited. Meetings with students of other Churches and ecclesial Communities can also be arranged.[98] Institutions for formation differ so much, however, that it is not possible to give uniform rules for this. As a matter of fact, reality allows for different nuances according to the diversity of nations and regions, as well as for difference of relations between the Catholic Church and the other Churches and ecclesial Communities on the level of ecclesiology, of collaboration and dialogue. Here also the necessity for gradualness and adaptation is very important and is unavoidable. Superiors must apply general principles and adapt these according to their particular situations and occasions.

2. Ministers and Collaborators not Ordained

a) Doctrinal Formation

83. Besides ordained ministers, there are other recognized collaborators in pastoral work—catechists, teachers and other lay helpers. Local Churches have institutes of religious science, pastoral institutes or other centres of formation or 'aggiornamento' for their formation. The same study programmes and norms as for the theological institutes apply here, but need to be adapted to the level of these participants and their studies.

84. More particularly, given the legitimate variety of charisms and of the work of monasteries, institutes of consecrated life, and societies of apostolic life, it is very important that "all communities should participate in the life of the Church. According to its individual character, each should make its own and foster in every possible way the enterprises and objectives of the Church", including the "ecumenical field".[99]

---

[98] Cf. nn. 192-194 below.
[99] Conciliar Decree *Perfectae Caritatis* (PC), n. 2.

Formation here should start in the novitiate and continue through the further stages. The *Ratio formationis* of the various institutes should, in analogy with the curricula of the ordained ministers, stress both an ecumenical dimension in every subject and provide for a specific course of ecumenism appropriately adapted to the circumstances and local situations. At the same time, it is important that the competent authority of the institute see to the formation of specialists in ecumenism to serve as guides for the ecumenical commitment of the whole institute.

b) ECUMENICAL EXPERIENCE

85. To translate study into experience, it is useful to encourage contacts and exchanges between Catholic monasteries and religious communities and those of other Churches and religious Communities. These can take the form of exchanges of information, spiritual or occasionally even material help, or can be in the form of cultural exchanges.

86. Given the importance of the role of the laity in the Church and in society, laity with ecumenical responsibilities should be encouraged to develop contacts and exchanges with other Churches and ecclesial Communities, in accordance with the norms of this Directory.[100]

C. SPECIALIZED FORMATION

87. *The importance of formation for dialogue.* Taking account of the influence of higher cultural institutes, it is clear that ecclesiastical faculties and other institutes of higher education play a specially important part in the preparation for and conduct of ecumenical dialogue and for progress towards that Christian unity which dialogue itself helps Christians to attain. Pedagogical preparation for dialogue must meet the following requirements:

a) a sincere personal commitment, lived out in faith, without which dialogue is no longer a dialogue between brothers and sisters but rather a mere academic exercise;

b) the search for new ways and means for building up mutual relationships and re-establishing unity based on greater fidelity to the Gos-

---

[100] Cf. nn. 50-51 above.

pel and on the authentic profession of the Christian faith, in truth and charity;

c) the conviction that ecumenical dialogue is not a purely private matter between persons or particular groups but that it takes place within the framework of the commitment of the whole Church and must in consequence be carried out in a way that is coherent with the teaching and the directives of its Pastors;

d) a readiness to recognize that the members of the different Churches and ecclesial Communities can help us better to understand and to expound accurately the doctrine and life of their Communities;

e) respect for the conscience and personal conviction of anyone who expounds an aspect or a doctrine of his or her own Church or its particular way of understanding Divine Revelation;

f) the recognition of the fact that not everybody is equally qualified to take part in dialogue, since there are various degrees of education, maturity of mind and spiritual progress.

The Role of the Ecclesiastical Faculties

88.   The Apostolic Constitution *Sapientia Christiana* lays down that in the first cycle of the theology faculty, fundamental theology should be studied with reference also to ecumenical questions.[101]

In the second cycle too, "ecumenical questions should be carefully treated, as directed by competent ecclesiastical authority".[102]

In other words, it will be opportune to give courses of specialization in ecumenism which, besides the elements indicated above in n. 79, could also deal with:

a) the present state of relations between the Catholic Church and the other Churches and ecclesial Communities, based on study of the published results of dialogue;

b) the study of the patrimony and traditions of other Christians, Eastern and Western;

[101] Cf. *SapC*, Practical Norms, art 51, 1, b.
[102] *SapC*, n. 69.

c) the importance in the ecumenical movement of the World Council of Churches and the present state of the Catholic Church's relations with the said Council;

d) the role of national and regional Councils of Churches, their achievements and difficulties.

It must also be remembered that the ecumenical dimension should also be present in theological teaching and research.

The Role of Catholic Universities

89. These too are called on to give sound ecumenical formation. Examples of the appropriate measures they may take are these:

a) to foster, when the subject calls for it, an ecumenical dimension to methods of teaching and research;

b) to organize discussions and study days on ecumenical questions;

c) to organize conferences and meetings for joint study, work and social activity, setting aside time for enquiry into Christian principles of social action and the means of putting them into practice. These occasions, whether involving only Catholics or bringing together Catholics and other Christians, should promote cooperation as far as possible with other advanced institutes in the area;

d) space could be given in university journals and reviews to reports on ecumenical events, and also to deeper ecumenical studies, with preference given to comments on the documents resulting from inter-church dialogue;

e) in academic halls of residence there is very much to recommend good relations between Catholics and other Christian students. With suitable guidance, they can learn, through these relations, to live together in a deeper ecumenical spirit and be faithful witnesses of their Christian faith;

f) it is important to give emphasis to prayer for unity, not only during the Week of Prayer for this purpose but also at other times during the year. Depending on circumstances of place and persons, and in conformity with the existing rules about shared worship, joint retreats under the guidance of a spiritual master, may also be envisaged;

g) there is a wide field of common witness in social or welfare works. Students should be trained and encouraged in this—not only theology students, but also those of other faculties, such as law, sociology and political science. By their contribution these students will help to promote and realize such initiatives;

b) chaplains, student counsellors and professors will have a particular concern to carry out their tasks in an ecumenical spirit, especially by organizing some of the initiatives indicated above. This obligation demands from them a deep knowledge of the doctrine of the Church, an adequate competence in academic subjects, unfailing prudence and a balanced attitude: all these qualities should enable them to help their students to harmonize their own life of faith with openness to others.

The Role of Specialized Ecumenical Institutes

90. To carry out its ecumenical task the Church needs a good number of experts in this matter—clerics, religious, lay men and women. These are necessary even in regions where Catholics are in the majority.

a) This calls for specialized institutes equipped with:
- — adequate documentation on ecumenism, especially on existing dialogues and future programmes;
- — and a staff of well-prepared and capable teachers both of Catholic doctrine and ecumenism.

b) These institutes should carry on ecumenical research in cooperation, as far as possible, with experts from other Christian traditions and their faithful; they should organize ecumenical meetings, such as conferences and congresses; and keep in touch with national ecumenical commissions and with the Pontifical Council for Promoting Christian Unity so as to be well informed and up to date with what is going on in interconfessional dialogue and with the progress accomplished.

c) Experts trained this way will supply personnel for the ecumenical task in order to promote the ecumenical movement in the Catholic Church, whether as members and directors of the responsible diocesan, national or international organisms, or as teachers of ecumenical subjects in institutes or ecclesiastical centres or as promoters of a genuine ecumenical spirit and action in their own surroundings.

91. Doctrinal formation and learning experience are not limited to the period of formation, but ask for a continuous "aggiornamento" of the ordained ministers and pastoral workers, in view of the continual evolution within the ecumenical movement.

Bishops and religious superiors, when organizing pastoral renewal programmes for clergy—through meetings, conferences, retreats, days of recollection or study of pastoral problems—should give careful attention to ecumenism along the following lines:

a) Systematic instruction of priests, religious, deacons and laity on the present state of the ecumenical movement, so that they may be able to introduce the ecumenical viewpoint into preaching, catechesis, prayer and Christian life in general. If it seems suitable and possible, it would be good to invite a minister of another Church to expound its tradition or speak on pastoral problems which are often common to all.

b) Where opportunity offers, and with the consent of the diocesan Bishop, Catholic clergy and those with pastoral responsibility in the diocese could take part in interconfessional meetings aimed at improving reciprocal relationships and at trying to resolve pastoral problems together. To give concrete form to these initiatives it might be useful to create local and regional clergy councils or associations, etc., or to join similar already existing societies.

c) Theology faculties and institutes of higher learning, as well as seminaries and other institutes of formation, can contribute to permanent formation, either by arranging courses for those involved in pastoral work, or by providing teachers or subsidies for the disciplines and courses organized by others.

d) Very useful also are the following: accurate information through the media of the local Church and, if possible, through the secular media; exchange of information with the media services of other Churches and ecclesial Communities; a permanent and systematic relationship with the diocesan and national ecumenical commission which will ensure precise and up to date documentation on ecumenical developments to all Catholics working in the field.

e) Full use should be made of the various kinds of spiritual meetings to explore those elements of spirituality which are held in common, as well as those which are particular. These meetings provide an opportunity to reflect on unity and to pray for the reconciliation of all Christians. The participation of members of different Churches and ecclesial Communities at such meetings can help to foster mutual understanding and the growth of spiritual communion.

f) Finally, it is desirable that an evaluation of ecumenical activity be made periodically.

IV

COMMUNION IN LIFE AND SPIRITUAL ACTIVITY AMONG THE BAPTIZED

A. THE SACRAMENT OF BAPTISM

92. By the sacrament of baptism a person is truly incorporated into Christ and into his Church and is reborn to a sharing of the divine life.[103] Baptism, therefore, constitutes the sacramental bond of unity existing among all who through it are reborn. Baptism, of itself, is the beginning, for it is directed towards the acquiring of fullness of life in Christ. It is thus ordered to the profession of faith, to the full integration into the economy of salvation, and to Eucharistic communion.[104] Instituted by the Lord himself, baptism, by which one participates in the mystery of his death and resurrection, involves conversion, faith, the remission of sin, and the gift of grace.

93. Baptism is conferred with water and with a formula which clearly indicates that baptism is done in the name of the Father, Son and Holy Spirit. It is therefore of the utmost importance for all the disciples of Christ that baptism be administered in this manner by all and that the various Churches and ecclesial Communities arrive as closely as possible at an agreement about its significance and valid celebration.

94. It is strongly recommended that the dialogue concerning both the significance and the valid celebration of baptism take place between Catholic authorities and those of other Churches and ecclesial Communities at the diocesan or Episcopal Conference levels. Thus it should be possible to arrive at common statements through which they express mutual recognition of baptisms as well as procedures for considering cases in which a doubt may arise as to the validity of a particular baptism.

[103] Cf. *UR*, n. 22.
[104] Cf. *ibidem*, n. 22.

95. In arriving at these expressions of common agreement, the following points should be kept in mind:

a) Baptism by immersion, or by pouring, together with the Trinitarian formula is, of itself, valid. Therefore, if the rituals, liturgical books or established customs of a Church or ecclesial Community prescribe either of these ways of baptism, the sacrament is to be considered valid unless there are serious reasons for doubting that the minister has observed the regulations of his/her own Community or Church.

b) The minister's insufficient faith concerning baptism never of itself makes baptism invalid. Sufficient intention in a minister who baptizes is to be presumed, unless there is serious ground for doubting that the minister intended to do what the Church does.

c) Wherever doubts arise about whether, or how water was used,[105] respect for the sacrament and deference towards these ecclesial Communities require that serious investigation of the practice of the Community concerned be made before any judgment is passed on the validity of its baptism.

96. According to the local situation and as occasion may arise, Catholics may, in common celebration with other Christians, commemorate the baptism which unites them, by renewing the engagement to undertake a full Christian life which they have assumed in the promises of their baptism, and by pledging to cooperate with the grace of the Holy Spirit in striving to heal the divisions which exist among Christians.

97. While by baptism a person is incorporated into Christ and his Church, this is only done in practice in a given Church or ecclesial Community. Baptism, therefore, may not be conferred jointly by two ministers belonging to different Churches or ecclesial Communities. Moreover, according to Catholic liturgical and theological tradition, baptism is celebrated by just one celebrant. For pastoral reasons, in particular circumstances the local Ordinary may sometimes permit, however, that a minister of another Church or ecclesial Community take part in the celebration by reading a lesson, offering a prayer, etc. Reciprocity is possible only if a baptism celebrated in another Community does not conflict with Catholic principles or discipline.[106]

---

[105] With regard to all Christians, consideration should be given to the danger of invalidity when baptism is administered by sprinkling, especially of several people at once.

[106] Cf. *Ecumenical Directory* (1967).

98. It is the Catholic understanding that godparents, in a liturgical and canonical sense, should themselves be members of the Church or ecclesial Community in which the baptism is being celebrated. They do not merely undertake a responsibility for the Christian education of the person being baptized (or confirmed) as a relation or friend; they are also there as representatives of a community of faith, standing as guarantees of the candidate's faith and desire for ecclesial communion.

> *a)* However, based on the common baptism and because of ties of blood or friendship, a baptized person who belongs to another ecclesial Community may be admitted as a witness to the baptism, but only together with a Catholic godparent.[107] A Catholic may do the same for a person being baptized in another ecclesial Community.

> *b)* Because of the close communion between the Catholic Church and the Eastern Orthodox Churches, it is permissible for a just cause for an Eastern faithful to act as godparent; together with a Catholic godparent, at the baptism of a Catholic infant or adult, so long as there is provision for the Catholic education of the person being baptized, and it is clear that the godparent is a suitable one.

A Catholic is not forbidden to stand as godparent in an Eastern Orthodox Church, if he/she is so invited. In this case, the duty of providing for the Christian education binds in the first place the godparent who belongs to the Church in which the child is baptized.[108]

99. Every Christian has the right for conscientious religious reasons, freely to decide to come into full Catholic communion.[109] The work of preparing the reception of an individual who wishes to be received into full communion with the Catholic Church is of its nature distinct from ecumenical activity.[110] The Rite of Christian Initiation of Adults provides a formula for receiving such persons into full Catholic communion. However, in such cases, as well as in cases of mixed marriages, the Catholic authority may consider it necessary to inquire as to whether the baptism already received was validly celebrated. The following recommendations should be observed in carrying out this inquiry.

---

[107] Cf. *CIC,* can. 874, 2. According to the explanation given by the *Acta Commissionis (Communicationes* 5, 1983, p. 182), the wording "communitas ecclesialis" does not include the Eastern Orthodox Churches not in full communion with the Catholic Church ("Notatur insuper Ecclesias Orientales Orthodoxas in schemate sub nomine communitatis ecclesialis non venire").

[108] Cf. *Ecumenical Directory* (1967), n. 48; *CCEO,* can. 685, 3.

[109] Cf. *UR,* n. 4; *CCEO,* cann. 896-901.

[110] Cf. *UR,* n. 4.

a) There is no doubt about the validity of baptism as conferred in the various Eastern Churches. It is enough to establish the fact of the baptism. In these Churches the sacrament of confirmation (chrismation) is properly administered by the priest at the same time as baptism. There it often happens that no mention is made of confirmation in the canonical testimony of baptism. This does not give grounds for doubting that this sacrament was also conferred.

b) With regard to Christians from other Churches and ecclesial Communities, before considering the validity of baptism of an individual Christian, one should determine whether an agreement on baptism (as mentioned above, n. 94) has been made by the Churches and ecclesial Communities of the regions or localities involved and whether baptism has in fact been administered according to this agreement. It should be noted, however, that the absence of a formal agreement about baptism should not automatically lead to doubt about the validity of baptism.

c) With regard to these Christians, where an official ecclesiastical attestation has been given, there is no reason for doubting the validity of the baptism conferred in their Churches and ecclesial Communities unless, in a particular case, an examination clearly shows that a serious reason exists for having a doubt about one of the following: the matter and form and words used in the conferral of baptism, the intention of an adult baptized or the minister of the baptism.[111]

d) If, even after careful investigation, a serious doubt persists about the proper administration of the baptism and it is judged necessary to baptize conditionally, the Catholic minister should show proper regard for the doctrine that baptism may be conferred only once by explaining to the person involved, both why in this case he is baptizing conditionally and what is the significance of the rite of conditional baptism. Furthermore, the rite of conditional baptism is to be carried out in private and not in public.[112]

e) It is desirable that Synods of Eastern Catholic Churches and Episcopal Conferences issue guidelines for the reception into full communion of Christians baptized into other Churches and ecclesial Communities. Account is to be taken of the fact that they are not catechumens and of the degree of knowledge and practice of the Christian faith which they may have.

[111] Cf. *CIC,* can. 869, 2, and n. 95 above.
[112] Cf. *CIC,* can. 869, 1 and 3.

100. According to the Rite of Christian Initiation of Adults, those adhering to Christ for the first time are normally baptized during the Paschal Vigil. Where the celebration of this Rite includes the reception into full communion of those already baptized, a clear distinction must be made between them and those who are not yet baptized.

101. In the present state of our relations with the ecclesial Communities of the Reformation of the 16th century, we have not yet reached agreement about the significance or sacramental nature or even of the administration of the sacrament of Confirmation. Therefore, under present circumstances, persons entering into full communion with the Catholic Church from one of these Communities are to receive the sacrament of Confirmation according to the doctrine and rite of the Catholic Church before being admitted to Eucharistic communion.

B. SHARING SPIRITUAL ACTIVITIES AND RESOURCES

General Principles

102. Christians may be encouraged to share in spiritual activities and resources, i.e., to share that spiritual heritage they have in common in a manner and to a degree appropriate to their present divided state.[113]

103. The term "sharing in spiritual activities and resources" covers such things as prayer offered in common, sharing in liturgical worship in the strict sense, as described below in n. 116, as well as common use of sacred places and of all necessary objects.

104. The principles which should direct this spiritual sharing are the following:

> *a*) In spite of the serious difficulties which prevent full ecclesial communion, it is clear that all those who by baptism are incorporated into Christ share many elements of the Christian life. There thus exists a real, even if imperfect, communion among Christians which can be expressed in many ways, including sharing in prayer and liturgical worship,[114] as will be indicated in the paragraph which follows.

[113] Cf. *UR*, n. 8.
[114] Cf. *UR*, nn. 3 and 8; see also n. 116 below.

b) According to Catholic faith, the Catholic Church has been endowed with the whole of revealed truth and all the means of salvation as a gift which cannot be lost.[115] Nevertheless, among the elements and gifts which belong to the Catholic Church (e.g.; the written Word of God, the life of grace, faith, hope and charity etc.) many can exist outside its visible limits. The Churches and ecclesial Communities not in full communion with the Catholic Church have by no means been deprived of significance and value in the mystery of salvation, for the Spirit of Christ has not refrained from using them as means of salvation.[116] In ways that vary according to the condition of each Church or ecclesial Community, their celebrations are able to nourish the life of grace in their members who participate in them and provide access to the communion of salvation.[117]

c) The sharing of spiritual activities and resources, therefore, must reflect this double fact:

1) the real communion in the life of the Spirit which already exists among Christians and is expressed in their prayer and liturgical worship;

2) the incomplete character of this communion because of differences of faith and understanding which are incompatible with an unrestricted mutual sharing of spiritual endowments.

d) Fidelity to this complex reality makes it necessary to establish norms for spiritual sharing which take into account the diverse ecclesial situations of the Churches and ecclesial Communities involved, so that, as Christians esteem and rejoice in the spiritual riches they have in common, they are also made more aware of the necessity of overcoming the separations which still exist.

e) Since Eucharistic concelebration is a visible manifestation of full communion in faith, worship and community life of the Catholic Church, expressed by ministers of that Church, it is not permitted to concelebrate the Eucharist with ministers of other Churches or ecclesial Communities.[118]

105.   There should be a certain "reciprocity" since sharing in spiritual activities and resources, even with defined limits, is a contribution, in a spirit of mutual good will and charity, to the growth of harmony among Christians.

---

[115] Cf. *LG*, n. 8; *UR*, n. 4.
[116] Cf. *UR*, n. 3.
[117] Cf. *UR*, nn. 3, 15, 22.
[118] Cf. *CIC*, can. 908; *CCEO*, can. 702.

106.   It is recommended that consultations on this sharing take place between appropriate Catholic authorities and those of other Communions to seek out the possibilities for lawful reciprocity according to the doctrine and traditions of different Communities.

107.   Catholics ought to show a sincere respect for the liturgical and sacramental discipline of other Churches and ecclesial Communities and these in their turn are asked to show the same respect for Catholic discipline. One of the objectives of the consultation mentioned above should be a greater mutual understanding of each other's discipline and even an agreement on how to manage a situation in which the discipline of one Church calls into question or conflicts with the discipline of another.

Prayer in Common

108.   Where appropriate, Catholics should be encouraged, in accordance with the Church's norms, to join in prayer with Christians of other Churches and ecclesial Communities. Such prayers in common are certainly a very effective means of petitioning for the grace of unity, and they are a genuine expression of the ties which still bind Catholics to these other Christians.[119] Shared prayer is in itself a way to spiritual reconciliation.

109.   Prayer in common is recommended for Catholics and other Christians so that together they may put before God the needs and problems they share—e.g., peace, social concerns, mutual charity among people, the dignity of the family, the effects of poverty, hunger and violence, etc. The same may be said of occasions when, according to circumstances, a nation, region or community wishes to make a common act of thanksgiving or petition to God, as on a national holiday, at a time of public disaster or mourning, on a day set aside for remembrance of those who have died for their country, etc. This kind of prayer is also recommended when Christians hold meetings for study or common action.

110.   Shared prayer should, however, be particularly concerned with the restoration of Christian unity. It can centre, e.g. on the mystery of the Church and its unity, on baptism as a sacramental bond of unity, or on the renewal of personal and community life as a necessary means to achieving unity. Prayer of this

---

[119] Cf. UR, n. 8.

type is particularly recommended during the "Week of Prayer for Christian Unity" or in the period between Ascension and Pentecost.

111. Representatives of the Churches, ecclesial Communities or other groups concerned should cooperate and prepare together such prayer. They should decide among themselves the way in which each is to take part, choose the themes and select the Scripture readings, hymns and prayers.

> *a*) In such a service there is room for any reading, prayer and hymn which manifest the faith or spiritual life shared by all Christian people. There is a place for an exhortation, address or biblical meditation drawing on the common Christian inheritance; and able to promote mutual good will and unity.

> *b*) Care should be taken that the versions of Holy Scripture used be acceptable to all and be faithful translations of the original text.

> *c*) It is desirable that the structure of these celebrations should take account of the different patterns of community prayer in harmony with the liturgical renewal in many Churches and ecclesial Communities, with particular regard being given to the common heritage of hymns, of texts taken from lectionaries and of liturgical prayers.

> *d*) When services are arranged between Catholics and those of an Eastern Church, particular attention should be given to the liturgical discipline of each Church, in accordance with n. 115 below.

112 Although a church building is a place in which a community is normally accustomed to celebrating its own liturgy, the common services mentioned above may be celebrated in the church of one or other of the communities concerned, if that is acceptable to all the participants. Whatever place is used should be agreeable to all, be capable of being properly prepared and be conducive to devotion.

113. Where there is a common agreement among the participants, those who have a function in a ceremony may use the dress proper to their ecclesiastical rank and to the nature of the celebration.

114. Under the direction of those who have proper formation and experience, it may be helpful in certain cases to arrange for spiritual sharing in the form of days of recollection, spiritual exercises, groups for the study and sharing of traditions of spirituality, and more stable associations for a deeper exploration of a common spiritual life. Serious attention must always be given to what has been said concerning the recognition of the real differences of doctrine which exist, as well as to the teaching and discipline of the Catholic Church concerning sacramental sharing.

115. Since the celebration of the Eucharist on the Lord's Day is the foundation and centre of the whole liturgical year,[120] Catholics—but those of Eastern Churches according to their own Law[121]—are obliged to attend Mass on that day and on days of precept.[122] It is not advisable therefore to organize ecumenical services on Sundays, and it must be remembered that even when Catholics participate in ecumenical services or in services of other Churches and ecclesial Communities, the obligation of participating at Mass on these days remains.

Sharing in Non-Sacramental Liturgical Worship

116. By liturgical worship is meant worship carried out according to books, prescriptions and customs of a Church or ecclesial Community, presided over by a minister or delegate of that Church or Community. This liturgical worship may be of a non-sacramental kind, or may be the celebration of one or more of the Christian sacraments. The concern here is non-sacramental worship.

117. In some situations, the official prayer of a Church may be preferred to ecumenical services specially prepared for the occasion. Participation in such celebrations as Morning or Evening Prayer, special vigils, etc., will enable people of different liturgical traditions—Catholic, Eastern, Anglican and Protestant—to understand each other's community prayer better and to share more deeply in traditions which often have developed from common roots.

118. In liturgical celebrations taking place in other Churches and ecclesial Communities, Catholics are encouraged to take part in the psalms, responses, hymns and common actions of the Church in which they are guests. If invited by their hosts, they may read a lesson or preach.

119. Regarding assistance at liturgical worship of this type, there should be a meticulous regard for the sensibilities of the clergy and people of all the Christian Communities concerned, as well as for local customs which may vary according to time, place, persons and circumstances. In a Catholic liturgical celebration, ministers of other Churches and ecclesial Communities may have the place and liturgical honors proper to their rank and their role, if this is judged desirable.

---

[120] Cf. *SC*, n. 106.
[121] Cf. *CCEO*, can. 881, 1; *CIC*, can. 1247.
[122] Cf. *CIC*, can. 1247; *CCEO*, can. 881, 1.

Catholic clergy invited to be present at a celebration of another Church or ecclesial Community may wear the appropriate dress or insignia of their ecclesiastical office, if it is agreeable to their hosts.

120. In the prudent judgment of the local Ordinary, the funeral rites of the Catholic Church may be granted to members of a non-Catholic Church or ecclesial Community, unless it is evidently contrary to their will and provided that their own minister is unavailable,[123] and that the general provisions of Canon Law do not forbid it.[124]

121. Blessings ordinarily given for the benefit of Catholics may also be given to other Christians who request them, according to the nature and object of the blessing. Public prayer for other Christians, living or dead, and for the needs and intentions of other Churches and ecclesial Communities and their spiritual heads may be offered during the litanies and other invocations of a liturgical service, but not during the Eucharistic Anaphora. Ancient Christian liturgical and ecclesiological tradition permits the specific mention in the Eucharistic Anaphora only of the names of persons who are in full communion with the Church celebrating the Eucharist.

Sharing in Sacramental Life, especially the Eucharist

a) *Sharing in Sacramental Life with members of the various Eastern Churches*

122. Between the Catholic Church and the Eastern Churches not in full communion with it, there is still a very close communion in matters of faith.[125] Moreover, "through the celebration of the Eucharist of the Lord in each of these Churches, the Church of God is built up and grows in stature" and "although separated from us, these Churches still possess true sacraments, above all—by apostolic succession—the priesthood and the Eucharist...".[126] This offers ecclesiological and sacramental grounds, according to the understanding of the Catholic Church, for allowing and even encouraging some sharing in liturgical worship, even of the Eucharist, with these Churches, "given suitable circumstances and the approval of church authorities".[127] It is recognized, however, that Eastern

---

[123] Cf. *CIC,* can. 1183, 3; *CCEO,* can. 876, 1.
[124] Cf. *CIC,* can. 1184; *CCEO,* can. 887.
[125] Cf. *UR,* n. 14.
[126] *Ibidem,* n. 15.
[127] *Ibidem.*

Churches, on the basis of their own ecclesiological understanding, may have more restrictive disciplines in this matter, which others should respect. Pastors should carefully instruct the faithful so that they will be clearly aware of the proper reasons for this kind of sharing in liturgical worship and of the variety of discipline which may exist in this connection.

123. Whenever necessity requires or a genuine spiritual advantage suggests, and provided that the danger of error or indifferentism is avoided, it is lawful for any Catholic for whom it is physically or morally impossible to approach a Catholic minister, to receive the sacraments of penance, Eucharist and anointing of the sick from a minister of an Eastern Church.[128]

124. Since practice differs between Catholics and Eastern Christians in the matter of frequent communion, confession before communion and the Eucharistic fast, care must be taken to avoid scandal and suspicion among Eastern Christians through Catholics not following the Eastern usage. A Catholic who legitimately wishes to communicate with Eastern Christians must respect the Eastern discipline as much as possible and refrain from communicating if that Church restricts sacramental communion to its own members to the exclusion of others.

125. Catholic ministers may lawfully administer the sacraments of penance, Eucharist and the anointing of the sick to members of the Eastern Churches, who ask for these sacraments of their own free will and are properly disposed. In these particular cases also, due consideration should be given to the discipline of the Eastern Churches for their own faithful and any suggestion of proselytism should be avoided.[129]

126. Catholics may read lessons at a sacramental liturgical celebration in the Eastern Churches if they are invited to do so. An Eastern Christian may be invited to read the lessons at similar services in Catholic churches.

127. A Catholic minister may be present and take part in the celebration of a marriage being properly celebrated between Eastern Christians or between a Catholic and an Eastern Christian in the Eastern church, if invited to do so by the Eastern Church authority and if it is in accord with the norms given below concerning mixed marriages, where they apply.

---

[128] Cf. *CIC*, can. 844, 2 and *CCEO*, can. 671, 2.
[129] Cf. *CIC*, can. 844, 3 and cf. n. 106 above.

128. A member of an Eastern Church may act as bridesmaid or best man at a wedding in a Catholic church; a Catholic also may be bridesmaid or best man at a marriage properly celebrated in an Eastern church. In all cases this practice must conform to the general discipline of both Churches regarding the requirements for participating in such marriages.

b) *Sharing Sacramental Life with Christians of Other Churches and Ecclesial Communities*

129. A sacrament is an act of Christ and of the Church through the Spirit.[130] Its celebration in a concrete community is the sign of the reality of its unity in faith, worship and community life. As well as being signs, sacraments—most specially the Eucharist—are sources of the unity of the Christian community and of spiritual life, and are means for building them up. Thus Eucharistic communion is inseparably linked to full ecclesial communion and its visible expression.

At the same time, the Catholic Church teaches that by baptism members of other Churches and ecclesial Communities are brought into a real, even if imperfect communion, with the Catholic Church [131] and that "baptism, which constitutes the sacramental bond of unity existing among all who through it are reborn... is wholly directed toward the acquiring of fullness of life in Christ".[132] The Eucharist is, for the baptized, a spiritual food which enables them to overcome sin and to live the very life of Christ, to be incorporated more profoundly in Him and share more intensely in the whole economy of the Mystery of Christ.

It is in the light of these two basic principles, which must always be taken into account together, that in general the Catholic Church permits access to its Eucharistic communion and to the sacraments of penance and anointing of the sick, only to those who share its oneness in faith, worship and ecclesial life.[133] For the same reasons, it also recognizes that in certain circumstances, by way of exception, and under certain conditions, access to these sacraments may be permitted, or even commended, for Christians of other Churches and ecclesial Communities.[134]

130. In case of danger of death, Catholic ministers may administer these sacraments when the conditions given below (n. 131) are present. In other cases, it is strongly recommended that the diocesan Bishop, taking into account any

---

[130] Cf. *CIC*, can. 840 and *CCEO*, can. 667.
[131] Cf. *UR*, n. 3.
[132] *UR*, n. 22.
[133] Cf. *UR*, n. 8; *CIC*, can. 844, 1 and *CCEO*, can. 671, 1.
[134] Cf. *CIC*, can. 844, 4 and *CCEO*, can. 671, 4.

norms which may have been established for this matter by the Episcopal Conference or by the Synods of Eastern Catholic Churches, establish general norms for judging situations of grave and pressing need and for verifying the conditions mentioned below (n. 131).[135] In accord with Canon Law,[136] these general norms are to be established only after consultation with at least the local competent authority of the other interested Church or ecclesial Community. Catholic ministers will judge individual cases and administer these sacraments only in accord with these established norms, where they exist. Otherwise they will judge according to the norms of this Directory.

131.   The conditions under which a Catholic minister may administer the sacraments of the Eucharist, of penance and of the anointing of the sick to a baptized person who may be found in the circumstances given above (n. 130) are that the person be unable to have recourse for the sacrament desired to a minister of his or her own Church or ecclesial Community, ask for the sacrament of his or her own initiative, manifest Catholic faith in this sacrament and be properly disposed.[137]

132.   On the basis of the Catholic doctrine concerning the sacraments and their validity, a Catholic who finds himself or herself in the circumstances mentioned above (nn. 130 and 131) may ask for these sacraments only from a minister in whose Church these sacraments are valid or from one who is known to be validly ordained according to the Catholic teaching on ordination.

133.   The reading of Scripture during a Eucharistic celebration in the Catholic Church is to be done by members of that Church. On exceptional occasions and for a just cause, the Bishop of the diocese may permit a member of another Church or ecclesial Community to take on the task of reader.

134.   In the Catholic Eucharistic Liturgy, the homily which forms part of the liturgy itself is reserved to the priest or deacon, since it is the presentation of the mysteries of faith and the norms of Christian living in accordance with Catholic teaching and tradition.[138]

---

[135] For the establishing of these norms we refer to the following documents: *On Admitting Other Christians to Eucharistic Communion in the Catholic Church* (1972) and *Note Interpreting the "Instruction on Admitting Other Christians to Eucharistic Communion Under Certain Circumstances"* (1973).

[136] Cf. *CIC*, can. 844, 5 and *CCEO*, can. 671, 5.

[137] Cf. *CIC*, can. 844, 4 and *CCEO*, can. 671, 4.

[138] Cf. *CIC*, can. 767 and *CCEO*, can. 614, 4.

135.   For the reading of Scripture and preaching during other than Eucharistic celebrations, the norms given above (n. 118) are to be applied.

136.   Members of other Churches or ecclesial Communities may be witnesses at the celebration of marriage in a Catholic church. Catholics may also be witnesses at marriages which are celebrated in other Churches or ecclesial Communities.

Sharing Other Resources for Spiritual Life and Activity

137.   Catholic churches are consecrated or blessed buildings which have an important theological and liturgical significance for the Catholic community. They are therefore generally reserved for Catholic worship. However, if priests, ministers or communities not in full communion with the Catholic Church do not have a place or the liturgical objects necessary for celebrating worthily their religious ceremonies, the diocesan Bishop may allow them the use of a church or a Catholic building and also lend them what may be necessary for their services. Under similar circumstances, permission may be given to them for interment or for the celebration of services at Catholic cemeteries.

138.   Because of developments in society, the rapid growth of population and urbanization, and for financial motives, where there is a good ecumenical relationship and understanding between the communities, the shared ownership or use of church premises over an extended period of time may become a matter of practical interest.

139.   When authorization for such ownership or use is given by the diocesan Bishop, according to any norms which may be established by the Episcopal Conference or the Holy See, judicious consideration should be given to the reservation of the Blessed Sacrament, so that this question is resolved on the basis of a sound sacramental theology with the respect that is due, while also taking account of the sensitivities of those who will use the building, e.g., by constructing a separate room or chapel.

140.   Before making plans for a shared building, the authorities of the communities concerned should first reach agreement as to how their various disciplines will be observed, particularly in regard to the sacraments. Furthermore, a written agreement should be made which will clearly and adequately take care of all questions which may arise concerning financial matters and the obligations arising from church and civil law.

141. In Catholic schools and institutions, every effort should be made to respect the faith and conscience of students or teachers who belong to other Churches or ecclesial Communities. In accordance with their own approved statutes, the authorities of these schools and institutions should take care that clergy of other Communities have every facility for giving spiritual and sacramental ministration to their own faithful who attend such schools or institutions. As far as circumstances allow, with the permission of the diocesan Bishop these facilities can be offered on the Catholic premises, including the church or chapel.

142. In hospitals, homes for the aged and similar institutions conducted by Catholics, the authorities should promptly advise priests and ministers of other Communities of the presence of their faithful and afford them every facility to visit these persons and give them spiritual and sacramental ministrations under dignified and reverent conditions, including the use of the chapel.

C. MIXED MARRIAGES

143. This section of the Ecumenical Directory does not attempt to give an extended treatment of all the pastoral and canonical questions connected with either the actual celebration of the sacrament of Christian marriage or the pastoral care to be given to Christian families, since such questions form part of the general pastoral care of every Bishop or regional Conference of Bishops. What follows below focuses on specific issues related to mixed marriages and should be understood in that context. The term "mixed marriage" refers to any marriage between a Catholic and a baptized Christian who is not in full communion with the Catholic Church.[139]

144. In all marriages, the primary concern of the Church is to uphold the strength and stability of the indissoluble marital union and the family life that flows from it. The perfect union of persons and full sharing of life which constitutes the married state are more easily assured when both partners belong to the same faith community. In addition, practical experience and the observations obtained in various dialogues between representatives of Churches and ecclesial Communities indicate that mixed marriages frequently present difficulties for the

[139] Cf. *CIC*, can. 1124 and *CCEO*, can. 813.

couples themselves, and for the children born to them, in maintaining their Christian faith and commitment and for the harmony of family life. For all these reasons, marriage between persons of the same ecclesial Community remains the objective to be recommended and encouraged.

145. In view, however, of the growing number of mixed marriages in many parts of the world, the Church includes within its urgent pastoral solicitude couples preparing to enter, or already having entered, such marriages. These marriages, even if they have their own particular difficulties, "contain numerous elements that could well be made good use of and develop both for their intrinsic value and for the contribution they can make to the ecumenical movement. This is particularly true when both parties are faithful to their religious duties. Their common baptism and the dynamism of grace provide the spouses in these marriages with the basis and motivation for expressing unity in the sphere of moral and spiritual values".[140]

146. It is the abiding responsibility of all, especially priests and deacons and those who assist them in pastoral ministry, to provide special instruction and support for the Catholic party in living his or her faith as well as for the couples in mixed marriages both in the preparation for the marriage, in its sacramental celebration and for the life together that follows the marriage ceremony. This pastoral care should take into account the concrete spiritual condition of each partner, their formation in their faith and their practice of it. At the same time, respect should be shown for the particular circumstances of each couple's situation, the conscience of each partner and the holiness of the state of sacramental marriage itself. Where judged useful, diocesan Bishops, Synods of Eastern Catholic Churches or Episcopal Conferences could draw up more specific guidelines for this pastoral care.

147. In fulfilling this responsibility, where the situation warrants it, positive steps should be taken, if possible, to establish contacts with the minister of the other Church or ecclesial Community, even if this may not always prove easy. In general, mutual consultation between Christian pastors for supporting such marriages and upholding their values can be a fruitful field of ecumenical collaboration.

148. In preparing the necessary marriage preparation programmes, the priest or deacon, and those who assist him, should stress the positive aspects of what

[140] Cf. *FC*, n. 78.

the couple share together as Christians in the life of grace, in faith, hope and love, along with the other interior gifts of the Holy Spirit.[141] Each party, while continuing to be faithful to his or her Christian commitment and to the practice of it, should seek to foster all that can lead to unity and harmony, without minimizing real differences and while avoiding an attitude of religious indifference.

149.   In the interest of greater understanding and unity, both parties should learn more about their partner's religious convictions and the teaching and religious practices of the Church or ecclesial Community to which he or she belongs. To help them live the Christian inheritance they have in common, they should be reminded that prayer together is essential for their spiritual harmony and that reading and study of the Sacred Scriptures are especially important. In the period of preparation, the couple's effort to understand their individual religious and ecclesial traditions, and serious consideration of the differences that exist, can lead to greater honesty, charity and understanding of these realities and also of the marriage itself.

150.   When, for a just and reasonable cause, permission for a mixed marriage is requested, both parties are to be instructed on the essential ends and properties of marriage which are not to be excluded by either party. Furthermore, the Catholic party will be asked to affirm, in the form established by the particular law of the Eastern Catholic Churches or by the Episcopal Conference, that he or she is prepared to avoid the dangers of abandoning the faith and to promise sincerely to do all in his/her power to see that the children of the marriage be baptized and educated in the Catholic Church. The other partner is to be informed of these promises and responsibilities.[142] At the same time, it should be recognized that the non-Catholic partner may feel a like obligation because of his/her own Christian commitment. It is to be noted that no formal written or oral promise is required of this partner in Canon Law.

Those who wish to enter into a mixed marriage should, in the course of the contacts that are made in this connection, be invited and encouraged to discuss the Catholic baptism and education of the children they will have, and where possible come to a decision on this question before the marriage.

In order to judge the existence or otherwise of a "just and reasonable cause" with regard to granting permission for this mixed marriage, the local Ordinary will take account, among other things, of an explicit refusal on the part of the non-Catholic party.

---

[141] Cf. *UR*, n. 3.
[142] Cf. *CIC*, cann. 1125, 1126 and *CCEO*, cann. 814, 815.

151. In carrying out this duty of transmitting the Catholic faith to the children, the Catholic parent will do so with respect for the religious freedom and conscience of the other parent and with due regard for the unity and permanence of the marriage and for the maintenance of the communion of the family. If, notwithstanding the Catholic's best efforts, the children are not baptized and brought up in the Catholic Church, the Catholic parent does not fall subject to the censure of Canon Law.[143] At the same time, his/her obligation to share the Catholic faith with the children does not cease. It continues to make its demands, which could be met, for example, by playing an active part in contributing to the Christian atmosphere of the home; doing all that is possible by word and example to enable the other members of the family to appreciate the specific values of the Catholic tradition; taking whatever steps are necessary to be well informed about his/her own faith so as to be able to explain and discuss it with them; praying with the family for the grace of Christian unity as the Lord wills it.

152. While keeping clearly in mind that doctrinal differences impede full sacramental and canonical communion between the Catholic Church and the various Eastern Churches, in the pastoral care of marriages between Catholics and Eastern Christians, particular attention should be given to the sound and consistent teaching of the faith which is shared by both and to the fact that in the Eastern Churches are to be found "true sacraments, and above all, by apostolic succession, the priesthood and the Eucharist, whereby they are still joined to us in closest intimacy".[144] If proper pastoral care is given to persons involved in these marriages, the faithful of both communions can be helped to understand how children born of such marriages will be initiated into and spiritually nourished by the sacramental mysteries of Christ. Their formation in authentic Christian doctrine and ways of Christian living would, for the most part, be similar in each Church. Diversity in liturgical life and private devotion can be made to encourage rather than hinder family prayer.

153. A marriage between a Catholic and a member of an Eastern Church is valid if it has taken place with the celebration of a religious rite by an ordained minister, as long as any other requirements of law for validity have been observed. For lawfulness in these cases, the canonical form of celebration is to be observed.[145] Canonical form is required for the validity of marriages between Catholics and Christians of Churches and ecclesial Communities.[146]

---

[143] Cf. *CIC*, can. 1366 and *CCEO*, can. 1439.
[144] Cf. *UR*, n. 15.
[145] Cf. *CIC*, can. 1127, 1 and *CCEO*, can. 834, 2.
[146] Cf. *CIC*, can. 1127, 1 and *CCEO*, can. 834, 1.

154. The local Ordinary of the Catholic partner, after having consulted the Local Ordinary of the place where the marriage will be celebrated, may for grave reasons and without prejudice to the law of the Eastern Churches,[147] dispense the Catholic partner from the observance of the canonical form of marriage.[148] Among these reasons for dispensation may be considered the maintaining of family harmony, obtaining parental consent to the marriage, the recognition of the particular religious commitment of the non-Catholic partner or his/her blood relationship with a minister of another Church or ecclesial Community. Episcopal Conferences are to issue norms by which such a dispensation may be granted in accordance with a common practice.

155. The obligation imposed by some Churches or ecclesial Communities for the observance of their own form of marriage is not a motive for automatic dispensation from the Catholic canonical form. Such particular situations should form the subject of dialogue between the Churches, at least at the local level.

156. One must keep in mind that, if the wedding is celebrated with a dispensation from canonical form, some public form of celebration is still required for validity.[149] To emphasize the unity of marriage, it is not permitted to have two separate religious services in which the exchange of consent would be expressed twice, or even one service which would celebrate two such exchanges of consent jointly or successively.[150]

157. With the previous authorisation of the local Ordinary, and if invited to do so, a Catholic priest or deacon may attend or participate in some way in the celebration of mixed marriages, in situations where the dispensation from canonical form has been granted. In these cases, there may be only one ceremony in which the presiding person receives the marriage vows. At the invitation of this celebrant, the Catholic priest or deacon may offer other appropriate prayers, read from the Scriptures, give a brief exhortation and bless the couple.

158. Upon request of the couple, the local Ordinary may permit the Catholic priest to invite the minister of the party of the other Church or ecclesial Community to participate in the celebration of the marriage, to read from the Scriptures, give a brief exhortation and bless the couple.

---

[147] Cf. *CCEO*, can. 835.
[148] Cf. *CIC*, can. 1127, 2.
[149] Cf. *CIC*, can. 1127, 2.
[150] Cf. *CIC*, can. 1127, 3 and *CCEO*, can. 839.

159. Because of problems concerning Eucharistic sharing which may arise from the presence of non-Catholic witnesses and guests, a mixed marriage celebrated according to the Catholic form ordinarily takes place outside the Eucharistic liturgy. For a just cause, however, the diocesan Bishop may permit the celebration of the Eucharist.[151] In the latter case, the decision as to whether the non-Catholic party of the marriage may be admitted to Eucharistic communion is to be made in keeping with the general norms existing in the matter both for Eastern Christians [152] and for other Christians,[153] taking into account the particular situation of the reception of the sacrament of Christian marriage by two baptized Christians.

160. Although the spouses in a mixed marriage share the sacraments of baptism and marriage, Eucharistic sharing can only be exceptional and in each case the norms stated above concerning the admission of a non-Catholic Christian to Eucharistic communion,[154] as well as those concerning the participation of a Catholic in Eucharistic communion in another Church,[155] must be observed.

---

[151] *Ordo celebrandi Matrimonium,* n. 8.
[152] Cf. n. 125 above.
[153] Cf. nn. 129-131 above.
[154] Cf. nn. 125, 130 and 131 above.
[155] Cf. n. 132 above.

V

ECUMENICAL COOPERATION
DIALOGUE AND COMMON WITNESS

161. When Christians live and pray together in the way described in Chapter IV, they are giving witness to the faith which they share and to their baptism, in the name of God, the Father of all, in his Son Jesus, the Redeemer of all, and in the Holy Spirit who transforms and unites all things through the power of love. Based on this communion of life and spiritual gifts, there are many other forms of ecumenical cooperation that express and promote unity and enhance the witness to the saving power of the Gospel that Christians give to the world. When Christians cooperate in studying and propagating the Bible, in liturgical studies, in catechesis and higher education, in pastoral care, in evangelization and in their service of charity to a world that is struggling to realize its ideals of justice and peace and love, they are putting into practice what was proposed in the Decree on Ecumenism:

> "Before the whole world, let all Christians profess their faith in God, one and three, in the incarnate Son of God, our Redeemer and Lord. United in their efforts, and with mutual respect, let them bear witness to our common hope, which does not play us false. Since in our times co-operation in social matters is very widely practiced, all without exception are summoned to united effort. Those who believe in God have a stronger summons, but the strongest claims are laid on Christians, since they have been sealed with the name of Christ. Cooperation among all Christians vividly expresses that bond which already unites them, and it sets in clearer relief the features of Christ the Servant".[156]

162. Christians cannot close their hearts to the crying needs of our contemporary world. The contribution they are able to make to all the areas of human life in which the need for salvation is manifested will be more effective when they make it together, and when they are seen to be united in making it. Hence they

---

[156] *UR*, n. 12.

will want to do everything together that is allowed by their faith. The absence of full communion between different Churches and ecclesial Communities, the divergences that still exist in teaching regarding both faith and morals, the wounded memories and the heritage of a history of separation—each of these set limits to what Christians can do together at this time. Their cooperation can help them to overcome the barriers to full communion and at the same time to put together their resources for building Christian life and service and the common witness that it gives, in view of the mission which they share:

> "In this unity in mission, which is decided principally by Christ himself, all Christians must find what already unites them even before their full communion is achieved."[157]

Forms and Structures of Ecumenical Cooperation

163. Ecumenical collaboration can take the form of participation by different Churches and ecclesial Communities in programmes already set up by one of their number. Or there may be a coordination of independent actions, with consequent avoidance of duplication and of the unnecessary multiplication of administrative structures. Or there may be joint initiatives and programmes. Various kinds of councils or committees may be set up, in more or less permanent form, to facilitate relations between Churches and ecclesial Communities and to promote cooperation and common witness among them.

164. Catholic participation in all forms of ecumenical meetings and cooperative projects should respect the norms established by the local ecclesiastical authority. Ultimately, it is for the diocesan Bishop, taking account of what has been decided at the regional or national level, to judge the acceptability and appropriateness of all forms of local ecumenical action. Bishops, Synods of Eastern Catholic Churches and Episcopal Conferences should act in accord with the directives of the Holy See and in a special way with those of the Pontifical Council for Promoting Christian Unity.

165. Meetings of authorized representatives of Churches and ecclesial Communities that occur periodically or on special occasions can help greatly to promote ecumenical cooperation. As well as being themselves an important witness to the commitment of those who participate in the promotion of Christian unity, they can give the stamp of authority to the cooperative efforts of members of the Churches and ecclesial Communities they represent. They may also provide the

---

[157] Pope John Paul II, Encyclical Letter *Redemptoris Hominis* (RH), n. 12.

occasion for examining what specific questions and tasks of ecumenical cooperation need to be addressed and for taking necessary decisions about the setting up of working groups or programmes to deal with them.

Councils of Churches and Christian Councils

166. Councils of Churches and Christian Councils are among the more permanent structures that are set up for promoting unity and ecumenical cooperation. A Council of Churches is composed of Churches [158] and is responsible to the Churches that set it up. A Christian Council is composed of other Christian groups and organizations as well as Churches. There are also other institutions for cooperation similar to these Councils but having other titles. Generally, Councils and similar institutions seek to enable their members to work together, to engage in dialogue, to overcome divisions and misunderstandings, to engage in prayer and work for unity, and to give, as far as possible, a common Christian witness and service. They are to be evaluated according to their activities and to the self-understanding set out in their constitutions. They have only the authority accorded to them by their constituent members. As a rule, they do not have responsibility for negotiations directed to the union of Churches.

167. Since it is desirable for the Catholic Church to find the proper expression for various levels of its relation with other Churches and ecclesial Communities, and since Councils of Churches and Christian Councils are among the more important forms of ecumenical cooperation, the growing contacts which the Catholic Church is having with Councils in many parts of the world are to be welcomed.

168. The decision to actually join a Council is the responsibility of the Bishops in the area served by the Council who also have responsibility for overseeing the Catholic participation in these Councils. For national Councils, that will generally be the Synod of Eastern Catholic Churches or the Episcopal Conference (except where there is only one diocese in a nation). In considering the question of membership of a Council, the appropriate authorities should be in touch during the preparation of the decision with the Pontifical Council for Promoting Christian Unity.

169. The pastoral advisability of joining a Council is one of the many factors that are to be taken into account in taking such a step. It must also be clear that

---

[158] In this context the term Church is generally to be understood in the sociological rather than in the strictly theological sense.

participation in the life of the Council can be compatible with the teaching of the Catholic Church, and does not blur its unique and specific identity. The first concern should be that of doctrinal clarity, especially as far as ecclesiology is concerned. Councils of Churches and Christian Councils do not in fact contain either within themselves or among themselves the beginning of a new Church which could replace the communion that now exists in the Catholic Church. They are not to proclaim themselves Churches or to claim for themselves an authority which would permit them to confer a ministry of Word or Sacrament.[159] Careful attention should be given to the Council's system of representation and voting rights, to its decision-making processes, to its manner of making public statements and to the degree of authority attributed to such statements. Clear and precise agreement on these matters should be reached before membership is taken up.[160]

170. Catholic membership of a local, national or regional Council is a quite distinct matter from the question of the relationship between the Catholic Church and the World Council of Churches. The World Council may, indeed, invite selected Councils "to enter into working relationships as associated Councils", but it does not have any authority or control over these Councils or their member Churches.

171. Joining a Council ought to be seen as undertaking serious responsibilities. The Catholic Church should be represented by well-qualified and committed persons. In the exercise of their mandate, they should be clearly aware of the limits beyond which they cannot commit the Church without referring the matter to the authority that has appointed them. The more attentively the work of these Councils is followed by their member Churches, the more important and efficacious will be the Councils' contribution to the ecumenical movement.

Ecumenical Dialogue

172. Dialogue is at the heart of ecumenical cooperation and accompanies all forms of it. Dialogue involves both listening and replying, seeking both to understand and to be understood. It is a readiness to put questions and to be questioned. It is to be forthcoming about oneself and trustful of what others say

---

[159] SPCU, *Ecumenical Collaboration at the Regional, National and Local Levels,* op.cit., n. 4 A.c.

[160] Episcopal Conferences and Synods of Eastern Catholic Churches should take care not to authorize Catholic participation in Councils of Churches in which groups are present who are not really considered to be ecclesial Communities.

76

about themselves. The parties in dialogue must be ready to clarify their ideas further, and modify their personal views and ways of living and acting, allowing themselves to be guided in this by authentic love and truth. Reciprocity and mutual commitment are essential elements in dialogue, as is also a sense that the partners are together on an equal footing.[161] Ecumenical dialogue allows members of different Churches and ecclesial Communities to get to know one another, to identify matters of faith and practice which they share and points on which they differ. They seek to understand the roots of such differences and assess to what extent they constitute a real obstacle to a common faith. When differences are recognised as being a real barrier to communion, they try to find ways to overcome them in the light of those points of faith which they already hold in common.

173. The Catholic Church may engage in dialogue at a diocesan level, at the level of Episcopal Conferences or Synods of Eastern Catholic Churches, and at the level of the universal Church. Its structure, as a universal communion in faith and sacramental life, allows it to present a consistent and united position on each of these levels. Where there is just one partner Church or Community in the dialogue, it is called bilateral; when there are several it is described as multilateral.

174. On the local level there are countless opportunities for exchanges between Christians, ranging from informal conversations that occur in daily life to sessions for the common examination in a Christian perspective of issues of local life or of concern to particular professional groups (doctors, social workers, parents, educators) and to study groups for specifically ecumenical subjects. Dialogues may be carried on by groups of lay people, by groups of clergy, by groups of professional theologians or by various combinations of these. Whether they have official standing (as a result of having been set up or formally authorized by ecclesiastical authority) or not, these exchanges must always be marked by a strong ecclesial sense. Catholics who take part in them will feel the need to be well informed about their faith and to deepen their living of it, and they will be careful to remain in communion of thought and desire with their Church.

175. The participants in certain dialogues are appointed by the hierarchy to take part not in a personal capacity, but as delegated representatives of their Church. Such mandates can be given by the local Ordinary, the Synod of Eastern Catholic Churches or the Episcopal Conference within its territory, or by the Holy See. In these cases, the Catholic participants have a special responsibility towards the authority that has sent them. The approval of that authority is also needed before any results of the dialogue engage the Church officially.

[161] Cf. *UR*, n. 9.

176. Catholic participants in dialogue follow the principles about Catholic doctrine set down by *Unitatis Redintegratio:*

> "The manner and order in which Catholic belief is expressed should in no way become an obstacle to dialogue with our brethren. It is, of course, essential that the doctrine be clearly presented in its entirety. Nothing is so foreign to the spirit of ecumenism as a false conciliatory approach which harms the purity of Catholic doctrine and obscures its assured genuine meaning.
>
> At the same time, Catholic belief needs to be explained more profoundly and precisely, in ways and in terminology which our separated brethren too can easily understand.
>
> Furthermore, Catholic theologians engaged in ecumenical dialogue, while standing fast by the teaching of the Church and searching together with separated brethren into the divine mysteries, should act with love for truth, with charity, and with humility. When comparing doctrines they should remember that in Catholic teaching there exists an order or 'hierarchy' of truths, since they vary in their relationship to the foundation of the Christian faith. Thus the way will be opened for this kind of fraternal rivalry to incite all to a deeper realization and a clearer expression of the unfathomable riches of Christ".[162]

The question of the hierarchy of truths is also taken up in the document *Reflections and Suggestions Concerning Ecumenical Dialogue:*

> "Neither in the life nor in the teaching of the whole Church is everything presented on the same level. Certainly all revealed truths demand the same acceptance of faith, but according to the greater or lesser proximity that they have to the basis of the revealed mystery, they are variously placed with regard to one another and have varying connections among themselves".[163]

177. The subject of dialogue may be a broad range of doctrinal issues covered over an extended period of time, or a single issue dealt with in a definite time framework; or it may be a pastoral or missionary problem about which the Churches wish to find a common position in order to eliminate conflicts that arise between them and to promote mutual help and common witness. For some questions a bilateral dialogue may be found more effective, for others multilateral dialogue gives better results. Experience shows that the two forms of dialogue complement one another in the complex task of promoting Christian unity. The

---

[162] *UR,* n. 11; cf. *Eph* 3:8.
[163] *Reflections and Suggestions* [...], op. cit. n. 4,b; cf. also *UR,* n. 11 and *ME,* n. 4. See also nn. 61a, 74-75 above and 181 below.

results of a bilateral dialogue should be promptly communicated to all other interested Churches or ecclesial Communities.

178.   A commission or committee set up to engage in dialogue on behalf of two or more Churches or ecclesial Communities may reach various degrees of agreement about the subject assigned to it and formulate their conclusions in a statement. Even before such agreement is reached, it may sometimes be judged useful by a commission to issue a statement or report that marks the convergencies that have been established, that identifies the problems that remain and suggests the direction that future dialogue might take. All statements or reports of dialogue commissions are submitted to the Churches concerned for assessment. Statements produced by dialogue commissions have intrinsic weight because of the competence and status of their authors. They are not, however, binding on the Catholic Church until they have been approved by the appropriate ecclesiastical authorities.

179.   When the results of a dialogue are considered by proper authorities to be ready for submission for evaluation, the members of the People of God, according to their role or charism, must be involved in this critical process. The faithful, as a matter of fact, are called to exercise: "the supernatural appreciation of the faith (*sensus fidei*) of the whole people, when 'from the Bishops to the last of the faithful' they manifest a universal consent in matters of faith and morals. By this appreciation of the faith, aroused and sustained by the Spirit of truth, the People of God, guided by the sacred teaching authority (*magisterium*), and obeying it, receives not the mere word of men, but truly the Word of God,[164] the faith once for all delivered to the saints.[165] The people unfailingly adheres to this faith, penetrates it more deeply with right judgment, and applies it more fully in daily life".[166]

Every effort should be made to find appropriate ways of bringing the results of dialogues to the attention of all members of the Church. In so far as possible, an explanation should be provided in respect of new insights into the faith, new witnesses to its truth, new forms of expression developed in dialogue—as well as with regard to the extent of the agreements being proposed. This will allow for an accurate judgment being made in respect of the reactions of all concerned as they assess the fidelity of these dialogue results to the Tradition of faith received from the Apostles and transmitted to the community of believers under the guidance of their authorized teachers. It is to be hoped that this manner of proceeding would be adopted by each Church or ecclesial Community that is

---

[164] Cf. *1 Thess.* 2:13.
[165] Cf. *Jude* 3.
[166] *LG*, n. 12.

partner to the dialogue and indeed by all Churches and ecclesial Communities that are hearing the call to unity. Cooperation between the Churches in this effort is most desirable.

180. The life of faith and the prayer of faith, no less than reflection on the doctrine of faith, enter into this process of reception, by which the whole Church, under the inspiration of the Holy Spirit "who distributes special graces among the faithful of every rank" [167] and guides in a special way the ministry of those who teach, makes its own the fruits of a dialogue, in a process of listening, of testing, of judging and of living.

181. In assessing and assimilating new forms of expression of the faith, which may appear in statements issued from ecumenical dialogue, or even ancient expressions which have been taken up again in preference to certain more recent theological terms, Catholics will bear in mind the distinction made in the Decree on Ecumenism between "the way that Church teaching has been formulated" and "the deposit of faith itself". [168] They will take care however to avoid ambiguous expressions especially in the search for agreement on points of doctrine that are traditionally controversial. They will also take account of the way in which the Second Vatican Council itself applied this distinction in its own formulation of Catholic faith; they must also allow for the "hierarchy of truths" in Catholic doctrine noted by the Decree on Ecumenism. [169]

182. The process of reception includes theological reflection of a technical nature on the Tradition of faith, as well as on the contemporary liturgical and pastoral reality of the Church. Important contributions to this process come from the specific competence of theological faculties. The whole process is guided by the official teaching authority of the Church which has the responsibility of making the final judgment about ecumenical statements. The new insights that are thus accepted enter into the life of the Church, renewing in a certain way that which fosters reconciliation with other Churches and ecclesial Communities.

Common Bible Work

183. The Word of God that is written in the Scriptures nourishes the life of the Church in manifold ways [170] and is "a precious instrument in the mighty hand

---

[167] *Ibidem.*
[168] Cf. *UR*, n. 6 and *GS*, n. 62.
[169] Cf. *UR*, n. 11.
[170] Cf. *DV*, chapter VI.

of God for attaining to that unity which the Saviour holds out to all men".[171] Veneration of the Scriptures is a fundamental bond of unity between Christians, one that holds firm even when the Churches and Communities to which they belong are not in full communion with each other. Everything that can be done to make members of the Churches and ecclesial Communities read the Word of God, and to do that together when possible (e.g., Bible Weeks), reinforces this bond of unity that already unites them, helps them to be open to the unifying action of God and strengthens the common witness to the saving Word of God which they give to the world. The provision and diffusion of suitable editions of the Bible is a prerequisite to the hearing of the Word. While the Catholic Church continues to produce editions of the Bible that meet its own specific standards and requirements, it also cooperates willingly with other Churches and ecclesial Communities in the making of translations and in the publication of common editions in accordance with what was foreseen by the Second Vatican Council and is provided for in the Code of Canon Law.[172] It sees ecumenical cooperation in this field as a valuable form of common service and common witness in the Church and to the world.

184. The Catholic Church is involved in this cooperation in many ways and at different levels. The Pontifical Council for Promoting Christian Unity was involved in the setting up, in 1969, of the World Catholic Federation for the Biblical Apostolate (now *"Catholic Biblical Federation)"*, as an international Catholic organization of a public character to further the pastoral implementation of *Dei Verbum,* ch. VI. In accordance with this objective, whenever local circumstances allow, collaboration at the level of local Churches as well as at regional level, between the ecumenical officer and the local sections of the Federation should be strongly encouraged.

185. Through the General Secretariat of the Catholic Biblical Federation, the Pontifical Council for Promoting Christian Unity maintains and develops relations with the United Bible Societies, an international Christian organization which has published jointly with the Secretariat *"Guidelines for Interconfessional Cooperation in Translating the Bible".*[173] This document sets out the principles, methods and concrete orientations of this special type of collaboration in the biblical field. This collaboration has already yielded good results. Similar contacts and cooperation between institutions devoted to the publication and use of the Bible are encouraged on all levels of the life of the Church. They can

---

[171] *UR,* n. 21.
[172] Cf. *CIC,* can. 825, 2 and *CCEO,* can. 655, 1.
[173] New revised edition 1987 of the first 1968 version. Published in *IS* of the Secretariat for Promoting Christian Unity, N 65 (1987) pp. 140-145.

help cooperation between the Churches and ecclesial Communities in missionary work, catechetics and religious education, as well as in common prayer and study. They can often result in the joint production of a Bible that may be used by several Churches and ecclesial Communities in a given cultural area, or for specific purposes such as study or liturgical life.[174] Cooperation of this kind can be an antidote to the use of the Bible in a fundamentalist way or for sectarian purposes.

186. Catholics can share the study of the Scriptures with members of other Churches and ecclesial Communities in many different ways and on many different levels. This sharing goes from the kind of work that can be done in neighbourhood or parochial groups to that of scholarly research among professional exegetes. In order to have ecumenical value, at whatever level it is done, this work needs to be grounded on faith and to nourish faith. It will often bring home to the participants how the doctrinal positions of different Churches and ecclesial Communities, and differences in their approaches to the use and exegesis of the Bible, lead to different interpretations of particular passages. It is helpful for Catholics when the editions of the Scriptures that they use actually draw attention to passages in which the doctrine of the Church is at issue. They will want to face up to any difficulties and disagreements that come from the ecumenical use of the Scriptures with an understanding of and a loyalty to the teaching of the Church. But this need not prevent them from recognizing how much they are at one with other Christians in the interpretation of the Scriptures. They will come to appreciate the light that the experience and traditions of the different Churches can throw on parts of the Scriptures that are especially significant for them. They will become more open to the possibility of finding new starting points in the Scriptures themselves for discussion about controversial issues. They will be challenged to discover the meaning of God's Word in relation to contemporary human situations that they share with their fellow Christians. Moreover, they will experience with joy the unifying power of God's Word.

Common Liturgical Texts

187. Churches and ecclesial Communities whose members live within a culturally homogeneous area should draw up together, where possible, a text of the most important Christian prayers (the Lord's Prayer, Apostles' Creed, Nice-

---

[174] In accordance with the norms laid down in *CIC,* cann. 825-827, 838 and in *CCEO,* cann. 655-659 and the *Decree* of the Sacred Congregation for the Doctrine of the Faith *Ecclesiae Pastorum* de Ecclesiae pastorum vigilantia circa Libros (19.3.1975) in *AAS* 1975, 281-184.

ne-Constantinopolitan Creed, a Trinitarian Doxology, the Glory to God in the Highest). These would be for regular use by all the Churches, and ecclesial Communities or at least for use when they pray together on ecumenical occasions. Agreement on a version of the Psalter for liturgical use, or at least of some of the more frequently used psalms would also be desirable; a similar agreement for common Scriptural readings for liturgical use should also be explored. The use of liturgical and other prayers that come from the period of the undivided Church can help to foster an ecumenical sense. Common hymn books, or at least common collections of hymns to be included in the hymn books of the different Churches and ecclesial Communities, as well as cooperation in developing liturgical music, are also to be recommended. When Christians pray together, with one voice, their common witness reaches to heaven as well as being heard on earth.

Ecumenical Cooperation in Catechesis

188. To complement the normal catechesis that Catholics must receive in any event, the Catholic Church recognizes that, in situations of religious pluralism, cooperation in the field of catechesis can enrich its own life as well as that of other Churches and ecclesial Communities. It can also strengthen their ability to give a common witness to the truth of the Gospel, in so far as this is possible. The basis of this cooperation, its conditions and its limits are set out in the Apostolic Exhortation *Catechesi Tradendae*:

> "Such experiences have a theological foundation in the elements shared by all Christians. But the communion of faith between Catholics and other Christians is not complete and perfect; in certain cases there are even profound divergences. Consequently, this ecumenical collaboration is by its very nature limited; it must never mean a 'reduction' to a common minimum. Furthermore, catechesis does not consist merely in the teaching of doctrine; it also means initiating into the whole of Christian life, bringing full participation in the sacraments of the Church. Therefore, where there is an experience of ecumenical collaboration in the field of catechesis, care must be taken that the education of Catholics in the Catholic Church should be well ensured in matters of doctrine and of Christian living".[175]

189. In some countries a form of Christian teaching common to Catholics and other Christians is imposed by the state or by particular circumstances, with

[175] N. 33.

text-books and the content of the course all laid down. In such cases, we are not dealing with true catechesis nor with books that can be used as catechisms. But such teaching, when it presents elements of Christian doctrine loyally, has authentic ecumenical value. In these cases, while appreciating the potential value of such teaching, it still remains indispensable to provide a specifically Catholic catechesis for Catholic children.

190. When the teaching of religion in schools is done in collaboration with members of religions other than Christian, a special effort should be made to ensure that the Christian message is presented in a way that highlights the unity of faith that exists between Christians about fundamental matters, while at the same time explaining the divisions that do exist and the steps that are being taken to overcome them.

Cooperation in Institutes of Higher Studies

191. There are many opportunities for ecumenical cooperation and common witness in the scientific study of theology and the branches of learning associated with it. Such cooperation contributes to theological research. It improves the quality of theological education by helping teachers to provide that attention to the ecumenical aspect of theological issues that is required in the Catholic Church by the conciliar decree *Unitatis Redintegratio*.[176] It facilitates the ecumenical formation of pastoral agents (see above chapter III). It helps Christians to address together the great intellectual issues that face men and women today from a shared fund of Christian wisdom and expertise. Instead of accentuating their difference they are able to give due preference to the profound harmony of faith and understanding that can exist within the diversity of their theological expressions.

In Seminaries and Undergraduate Studies.

192. Ecumenical cooperation in study and teaching is already desirable in programmes of the first stages of theological education, such as are given in seminaries and in first cycles of theological faculties. This cannot yet be done in the same way as is possible at the level of research and among those who have already completed their basic theological formation. An elementary requirement for ecumenical cooperation at those higher levels—to be dealt with in nn. 196-203 -, is that the participants be well formed in their faith and in the tradition of their own Church. Theological education in seminaries and first-cycle

[176] Cf. *UR*, nn. 10-11.

courses is directed to giving students this basic formation. The Catholic Church, like other Churches and ecclesial Communities, plans the programmes and courses that it considers appropriate for this purpose and selects suitably qualified directors and professors. The rule is that professors of the doctrinal courses should be Catholics. Thus the elementary principles of initiation into ecumenism and ecumenical theology, which is a necessary part of basic theological formation, are given by Catholic teachers.[177] Once these fundamental concerns of the Church about the purpose, values and requirements of initial theological training—which are understood and shared by many other Churches and ecclesial Communities—are respected, students and teachers from Catholic seminaries 'and theological faculties can cooperate ecumenically in various ways.

193. The norms for promoting and regulating cooperation between Catholics and other Christians at the level of seminary and first cycle theological studies are to be determined by Synods of Eastern Catholic Churches and Episcopal Conferences, particularly in so far as they affect the education of candidates for ordination. The appropriate ecumenical commission should be heard on the subject. The relevant guidelines should be included in the Programme of Training for Priesthood that is drawn up in accordance with the Decree on the Training of Priests *Optatam Totius*. Since institutes for training members of religious orders may also be involved in this kind of ecumenical cooperation in theological education, major superiors or their delegates should contribute towards drawing up rules, in keeping with the Conciliar Decree *Christus Dominus*.[178]

194. Catholic students may attend special courses given at institutes, including seminaries, of Christians of other Churches and ecclesial Communities, in accordance with the general criteria for the ecumenical formation of Catholic students, and subject to any norms that may have been laid down by the Synod of Eastern Catholic Churches or the Episcopal Conference. When a decision has to be taken about whether or not they should actually attend special courses, attention will be paid to the usefulness of the course in the general context of their training, the quality and ecumenical attitude of the professor, the level of previous preparation of the pupils themselves, as well as their spiritual and psychological maturity. The more closely the lectures or courses bear on doctrinal subjects, the more care will be needed in coming to a decision regarding the participation of the students. The formation of students and the development of their ecumenical sense is to be undertaken by a gradual process.

[177] Cf. n. 72 above and Circular Letter of the SPCU on Ecumenical Teaching, n. 6, in *IS*, n. 62 (1986), p. 196.
[178] Cf. *CD*, n. 35, 5-6.

195. In the second and third cycles of faculties and in seminaries after the students have received basic formation, professors from other Churches and ecclesial Communities may be invited to give lectures on the doctrinal positions of the Churches and Communities they represent, in order to complete the ecumenical formation the students are already receiving from their Catholic professors. Such professors may also provide courses of a technical nature, as for example, language courses, instruction on communication media, religious sociology, etc. In laying down norms to regulate this matter, Synods of Eastern Catholic Churches and Episcopal Conferences will bear in mind the degree of development reached by the ecumenical movement in their country and the state of relationship between Catholics and other Churches and ecclesial Communities. [179] They will specifically determine how Catholic criteria concerning the qualifications of professors, the period of their teaching and their accountability for the content of courses [180] are to be applied in their region. They will also give directives about how the teaching received by Catholic students in such lectures can be integrated into their complete programme. Professors so invited will be classified as "visiting lecturers". When necessary, Catholic institutions will organize seminars or courses to put into context the teaching given by lecturers from other Churches and ecclesial Communities. Catholic professors invited to lecture in corresponding circumstances in the seminaries and theological schools of other Churches and ecclesial Communities will gladly do so under the same conditions. Such an exchange of professors, that respects the concerns of each Church and ecclesial Community for the basic theological formation of its members, and especially of those who are called to be its ministers, is an effective form of ecumenical collaboration and gives an appropriate witness to Christian concern for sound teaching in the Church of Christ.

In Theological Research and Post-Graduate Studies.

196. A wider field of ecumenical collaboration is open to those who are engaged in theological research and teaching on a post-graduate level than is possible on the level of seminary or undergraduate (institutional) teaching. The maturity of the participants (research workers, professors, students) and the advanced levels of study already attained in the faith and theology of their own Church brings a special security and richness to their cooperation, such as could not be expected from those who are still engaged in undergraduate or seminary formation.

197. Cooperation in higher studies is practised by experts who consult and share their research with experts from other Churches and ecclesial Communi-

---

[179] Cf. SPCU, *Circular Letter on Ecumenical Teaching,* 10a, op. cit., p. 197.
[180] Cf. *Ibidem.*

ties. It is practised by ecumenical groups and associations of experts set up for the purpose. It is to be found in a special way within various forms of relationships that are entered into between institutions for the study of theology that belong to different Churches and ecclesial Communities. Such relationships and the cooperation they facilitate can help to give an ecumenical character to all the work of the participating institutions. They can provide for a sharing of personnel, library, courses, premises and other resources, to the considerable advantage of researchers, professors and students.

198.   Ecumenical cooperation is particularly indicated in the interest of those institutes that are set up within existing faculties of theology for research and specialized formation in ecumenical theology or for the pastoral practice of ecumenism; it can similarly benefit those independent institutes that are set up for the same purpose. Although these latter may belong to particular Churches or ecclesial Communities, they will be more effective when they cooperate actively with similar institutes that belong to other Churches. It may be useful from an ecumenical point of view if such institutes have members of other Churches and ecclesial Communities on their staff and in their student body.

199.   The setting up and administration of institutions and structures for ecumenical collaboration in the study of theology should normally be entrusted to those who conduct the institutions involved, and to those who work within them in a spirit of legitimate academic freedom. Their ecumenical effectiveness requires that they operate in close relationship with the authorities of the Churches and ecclesial Communities to which their members belong. When the institute involved in such cooperative structures is part of a faculty of theology that already belongs to the Catholic Church, or is set up by it as a separate institution under its authority, its relationship to Church authorities in ecumenical activity will be defined in the articles of agreement on cooperation.

200.   Interconfessional institutes, set up and administered jointly by several Churches and ecclesial Communities, are especially effective in dealing with topics of common concern to all Christians. Joint study of certain questions will indeed contribute to the solution of problems and to the approval of suitable policies, thus contributing to the advancement of Christian unity. Among such questions the following may be mentioned: mission work, relations with non-Christian religions, atheism and unbelief, the use of social communications media, architecture and sacred art, theological subjects as the explanation of Holy Scripture, salvation history and pastoral theology. The responsibility of such institutes towards the authorities of the Churches and ecclesial Communities concerned is to be defined clearly in their statutes.

201. Associations or institutes may be set up for the joint study of theological and pastoral questions by ministers of different Churches and ecclesial Communities. Under the guidance and with the help of experts in various fields, these ministers discuss and analyse together the theoretical and practical aspects of their ministry within their own Communities, in its ecumenical dimensions and in its contribution to common Christian witness.

202. The field of study and research in institutes for ecumenical activity and cooperation can cover the whole ecumenical reality, or it can be limited to particular questions that are studied in depth. When institutes specialize in the study of one area of ecumenism (the Orthodox tradition, Protestantism, the Anglican Communion, as well as the kind of questions mentioned in n. 200), it is important that they should deal with that study within the context of the whole ecumenical movement and all the other questions that are connected with the subject under consideration.

203. Catholic institutions are encouraged to become members of ecumenical associations designed to promote improvement in the standard of theological education, better training of those intended for pastoral ministry and better co-operation between institutions for advanced learning. They will be also open to proposals that are being put forward with increasing frequency today by the authorities of public and non-denominational universities to bring together for the study of religion different institutes that are connected with them. Membership of such ecumenical associations and participation in the teaching of associated institutes must respect the legitimate autonomy of Catholic institutes in matters of the programme of studies, of the doctrinal content of subjects to be taught, and of the spiritual and priestly training of students destined for ordination.

Pastoral Cooperation in Special Situations

204. While each Church and ecclesial Community takes pastoral care of its own members and is built up in an irreplaceable way by the ministers of its local communities, there are certain situations in which the religious need of Christian people may well be served more effectively when pastoral agents, ordained or lay, from different Churches and ecclesial Communities work together. This kind of ecumenical collaboration can be practised with success in the pastoral care of those who are in hospitals, prisons, the armed forces, universities, and large industrial complexes. It is also effective in bringing a Christian presence into the world of the social communications media. Care should be taken to coordinate these special ecumenical ministries with the local pastoral structures of each Church. That will be more readily achieved when those structures are themselves imbued with the ecumenical spirit and practise ecumenical cooperation with corresponding local units of other Churches or ecclesial Communities. Liturgical ministry, especially that of the Eucharist and of the other sacraments, is provided in such cooperative situations according to the norms that each Church or ecclesial Community lays down for its own members, which for Catholics are those stated in chapter IV of this Directory.

Cooperation in Missionary Activity

205. The common witness given by all forms of ecumenical cooperation is already missionary. The ecumenical movement has, in fact, gone hand in hand with a new discovery by many communities of the missionary nature of the Church.

Ecumenical cooperation shows to the world that those who believe in Christ and live by his Spirit, being thus made children of God who is Father of all, can set about over coming human divisions, even about such sensitive matters as religious faith and practice, with courage and hope. The divisions that exist among Christians are certainly a major obstacle to the successful preaching of the Gospel.[181] But the efforts being made to overcome them do much to offset the scandal and to give credibility to Christians who proclaim that Christ is the one in whom all things and people are gathered together into unity:

> "As evangelizers we must offer Christ's faithful not the image of people divided and separated by unedifying quarrels, but the image of people who are mature in faith and capable of finding a meeting-point beyond the real tensions, thanks to a shared, sincere and disinterested search for truth. Yes, the destiny of evangelization is certainly bound up with the witness of unity given by the Church. This is a source of responsibility and also of comfort".[182]

206. Ecumenical witness can be given in missionary activity itself. For Catholics, the basis for ecumenical cooperation with other Christians in mission is "the foundation of baptism and the patrimony of faith which is common to us".[183] Other Churches and ecclesial Communities which draw people to faith in Christ the Saviour and to baptism in the name of the Father, Son and Holy Spirit draw

---

[181] Cf. *UR*, n. 1.
[182] *EN*, n. 77.
[183] *Ibidem*.

them into the real though imperfect communion that exists between them and the Catholic Church. Catholics would want all who are called to Christian faith to join with them in that fullness of communion they believe to exist in the Catholic Church, yet they recognize that in the Providence of God some will live out their Christian lives in Churches and ecclesial Communities that do not provide such full communion. They should be careful to respect the lively faith of other Churches and ecclesial Communities which preach the Gospel, and rejoice in the grace of God that is at work among them.

207. Catholics can join with other Churches and ecclesial Communities —provided there is nothing sectarian or deliberately anti-Catholic about their work of evangelization—in organizations and programmes that give common support to the missionary activities of all the participating Churches. A special subject of such cooperation will be to ensure that the human, cultural and political factors that were involved in the original divisions between the Churches, and have marked the historical tradition of separation, will not be transplanted into areas where the Gospel is being preached and Churches are being founded. Those who have been sent by missionary institutes to help in the foundation and growth of new Churches, will be especially sensitive to this need. Bishops will give special attention to it. It is for the Bishop to determine when it becomes necessary to insist in a special way on points of doctrine and morality about which Catholics differ from other Churches and ecclesial Communities. These latter may find it necessary to do the same in relation to Catholicism. But all this must be done, not in a contentious or sectarian spirit, but with mutual respect and love.[184] New converts to the faith should be carefully nourished in the ecumenical spirit, "so that, while avoiding every form of indifferentism or confusion and also senseless rivalry, Catholics might collaborate with their separated brethren, insofar as it is possible, by a common profession before the nations of faith in God and in Jesus Christ, and by a common, fraternal effort in social, cultural, technical and religious matters".[185]

208. Ecumenical cooperation is particularly necessary in the mission to the de-Christianized masses of our contemporary world. The ability of Christians, though still divided, to bear common witness, even now, to central truths of the Gospel [186] can be a powerful invitation to a renewed appreciation of Christian faith in a secularized society. A common evaluation of the forms of atheism, secularization and materialism that are at work in the world of today, and a shared strat-

---

[184] Cf. *AG,* n. 6.
[185] *Ibidem,* n. 15.
[186] Cf. *RH,* n. 11.

egy to deal with them would greatly benefit the Christian mission to the contemporary world.

209. There should be a special place for cooperation between members of the different Churches and ecclesial Communities in the reflection constantly needed on the meaning of Christian mission, on the manner of engaging in the dialogue of salvation with the members of other religions and on the general question of the relationship between the preaching of the Gospel of Christ and the cultures and way of thinking of the contemporary world.

Ecumenical Cooperation in the Dialogue with Other Religions

210. There are increasing contacts in today's world between Christians and persons of other religions. These contacts differ radically from the contacts between the Churches and ecclesial Communities, which have for their object the restoration of the unity Christ willed among all his disciples and are properly called ecumenical. But in practice they are deeply influenced by, and in turn influence ecumenical relationships. Through them Christians can deepen the level of communion existing among themselves, and so they are to be considered an important part of ecumenical cooperation. This is particularly true for all that is done to develop the specially privileged religious relationship that Christians have with the Jewish people.

For Catholics, directives about relationships with the Jewish people are guided by the Commission for Religious Relations with the Jews. Relations with the members of other religions are guided by the Pontifical Council for Inter-Religious Dialogue. In working out religious relationships with Jews and in their relations with members of other religions, in accordance with appropriate directives, Catholics can find many opportunities for collaboration with members of other Churches and ecclesial Communities. There are many areas where Christians can work together in fostering dialogue and common action with the Jews, as for example in struggling together against anti-Semitism, religious fanaticism and sectarianism. Collaboration with other believers can take place in promoting religious perspectives on issues of justice and peace, support for family life, respect for minority communities, and such cooperation can also address the many new questions of the present age. In these interreligious contacts, Christians can appeal together to their common biblical and theological sources, thereby bringing Christian insights to this broader context, in a way that fosters Christian unity as well.

Ecumenical Cooperation in Social and Cultural Life

211. The Catholic Church considers ecumenical collaboration in social and cultural life to be an important aspect of working towards unity. The Decree on Ecumenism sees such cooperation as a clear expression of the bond that unites all the baptized.[187] For this reason, it encourages and supports very concrete forms of collaboration:

> "Such cooperation which has already begun in many countries, should be ever increasingly developed, particularly in regions where a social and technical evolution is taking place. It should contribute to a just appreciation of the dignity of the human person, the promotion of the blessings of peace, the application of Gospel principles to social life, and advancement of the arts and science in a Christian spirit. Christians should also work together in the use of every possible means to relieve the afflictions of our times such as famine and national disasters, illiteracy and poverty, lack of housing, and the unequal distribution of wealth".[188]

212. As a general principle, ecumenical collaboration in the social and cultural life ought to be carried out within the overall context of the search for Christian unity. When it is not accompanied by other forms of ecumenism, especially by prayer and spiritual sharing, it can easily be confused with ideological and merely political interests and thus become an obstacle to the progress toward unity. Like all forms of ecumenism, it should be carried out under the supervision of the local Ordinary, the Episcopal Conference or the Synod of the Eastern Catholic Churches.

213. Through such cooperation, all believers in Christ are able to learn easily how they can understand each other better and esteem each other more, and so prepare the way for the unity of Christians.[189] On a number of occasions, Pope John Paul II has affirmed the commitment of the Catholic Church to ecumenical collaboration.[190] The same affirmation was expressed in the common declaration between Cardinal Johannes Willebrands and Dr. Philip Potter, General Secretary of the World Council of Churches, on the occasion of the Holy Father's visit to

---

[187] Cf. *UR*, n. 12
[188] *Ibidem.*
[189] Cf. *Ibidem.*
[190] Cf. Pope John Paul II, *Address* to the Roman Curia, 28 June 1985, *AAS* 1985, 1148-1159; cf. idem Encyclical Letter *Sollicitudo Rei Socialis* (SRS), n. 32.

the World Council of Churches' headquarters in Geneva in 1984.[191] It is in view of this that the Ecumenical Directory offers some examples of collaboration at various levels without these pretending to be exhaustive in any way.[192]

a) *Cooperation in common studies of social and ethical questions*

214. Regional or national Episcopal Conferences, in collaboration with other Churches and ecclesial Communities, as well as with Councils of Churches, could set up groups to give common expression to basic Christian and human values. This kind of shared discernment will help to provide a significant starting point for an ecumenical address to questions of a social and ethical nature; it will open up the moral and social dimension of the partial communion that Christians of different Churches and ecclesial Communities already enjoy.

The purpose of a common study of this kind is the promotion of a Christian culture, a "civilization of love"—the Christian humanism often spoken of by Pope Paul VI and Pope John Paul II. To construct this culture, we must clearly establish the values that form part of it as well as the things that threaten it. Clearly, therefore, the study will involve for example a Christian appreciation of the value of life, the meaning of human work, questions of justice and peace, religious liberty, human rights and land rights. It will likewise focus on the factors in society that threaten basic values, such as poverty, racism, consumerism, terrorism, and indeed all that threatens human life at whatever stage of its development. The long tradition of Catholic social teaching will provide considerable guidance and inspiration for this kind of collaboration.

b) *Cooperation in the field of development, human need and stewardship of creation*

215. There is an intrinsic connection between development, human need and the stewardship of creation. For experience has taught us that development in response to human needs cannot misuse or overuse natural resources without serious consequences.

The responsibility for the care of creation, which in itself has a particular dignity, is given by the Creator himself to all people, in so far as they are to be stewards of creation.[193] Catholics are encouraged to enter, at various levels, into joint initiatives aimed at study and action on issues that threaten the dignity of creation and endanger the whole human race. Other topics for such study and

[191] Cf. SPCU, *IS*, 55, 1984, pp. 42-43.
[192] *Ecumenical Collaboration [...]*, op.cit. n. 3.
[193] *RH*, nn. 8, 15, 16; *SRS*, nn. 26, 34.

action could include, for example, certain forms of uncontrolled rapid industrialization and technology that cause pollution of the natural environment with serious consequences to the ecological balance, such as destruction of forests, nuclear testing and the irrational use or misuse of both renewable and unrenewable natural resources. An important aspect of joint action in this field is in the area of education of people in the use of resources as well as in the planned use of them and in the care of creation.

The field of development, which is basically a response to human needs, offers a variety of possibilities for collaboration between the Catholic Church and Churches and ecclesial Communities at regional, national and local levels. Such collaboration would include, among other things, working for a more just society, for peace, for promotion of the rights and dignity of women, and for a more equitable distribution of resources. In this sense, it would be possible to provide joint services for the poor, the sick, the handicapped, the aged and all who suffer because of unjust "structures of sin".[194] Cooperation in this field is encouraged particularly in places where there is high concentration of population with serious consequences for housing, food, water, clothing, sanitation and medical care. An important aspect of collaboration in this field would be in dealing with the problem of migrants, refugees, and victims of natural catastrophes. In the event of world emergencies, the Catholic Church encourages the pooling of resources and services with the international organizations of Churches and ecclesial Communities, for reasons of efficiency and to reduce costs. It likewise encourages ecumenical collaboration with international organizations that specialize in these concerns.

c) *Cooperation in the field of medicine*

216. The whole area of health care constitutes a very important challenge for ecumenical collaboration. In some countries ecumenical collaboration by the Churches in health care programmes is vital if adequate health care is to be provided. Increasingly, moreover, collaboration in this whole area, be it at the level of research, or at the level of practical health care, raises questions of medical ethics which are both a challenge and an opportunity for ecumenical collaboration. The task mentioned earlier of identifying basic values that are integral to Christian life is especially urgent, given the rapid developments in areas such as genetics. In this context, the indications of the 1975 document on ecumenical collaboration [195] are especially pertinent: "Particularly where ethical norms are con-

---

[194] *SRS*, n. 36.
[195] Cf. *op. cit.*, n. 3 g.

cerned, the doctrinal stand of the Catholic Church has to be made clear and the difficulties which this can raise for ecumenical collaboration faced honestly and with loyalty to Catholic teaching".

d) *Cooperation in Social Communications Media*

217.   It is possible to cooperate in this matter, in understanding the nature of modern media and particularly the challenges it offers to Christians today. Collaboration in this area could include ways of infusing Christian principles into communications media and study of problems encountered in this field, as well as education of the people on critical use of the media. Interconfessional groups can be especially effective as advisory bodies to the secular media, particularly as to the way in which they deal with religious affairs. This can be particularly useful in countries where the majority of viewers, listeners, or readers are from one particular Church or ecclesial Community. "There is almost no end to the opportunities for such collaboration. Some are obvious: joint programmes on radio and television; educational projects and services, especially for parents and young people; meetings and discussions between professionals on an international level; recognition of achievement in these fields by annual awards; cooperation in research in the media field and especially in professional training and education".[196] Where interconfessional structures with full Catholic participation already exist, they should be strengthened, particularly for the use of radio and television, and for publishing and audio-visual work. At the same time, each participating body should be given the opportunity to enunciate its own doctrine and practice.[197]

218.   It would be important at times to work in mutual cooperation; either by having Catholic communicators take part in the initiatives of other Churches and ecclesial Communities, or by having communicators from these latter to participate in Catholic initiatives. Ecumenical collaboration could include exchanges between International Catholic Organizations and the communications organizations of other Churches and ecclesial Communities (as, for example, in keeping the World Day for Social Communications). The common use of satellites and cable television networks offers practical opportunities for ecumenical collaboration.[198] Clearly, at the regional level, this kind of collaboration should take place with reference to ecumenical commissions and, internationally, with reference to

---

[196] Pontifical Council for Social Communications, Pastoral Instruction *Communio et Progressio*, n. 99, *AAS* 1971, 593-656.

[197] Cf. *Ecumenical Collaboration [...]*, op cit., 3, f.

[198] Cf. Pontifical Council for Social Communications, *Criteria for Ecumenical and Interreligious Cooperation in Communications*, nn. 11 and 14, 1989, *Origins*, 1989, n. 23, 375-377.

the Pontifical Council for Promoting Christian Unity. The formation of Catholic communicators should include a serious ecumenical preparation.

On March 25th, 1993, His Holiness Pope John Paul II approved this Directory, confirmed it by his authority and ordered that it be published. Anything to the contrary notwithstanding.

EDWARD IDRIS CARDINAL CASSIDY
President

✠ PIERRE DUPREY
Tit. Bishop of Thibar
Secretary